THE AMNESIA FACTOR

J. H. MATHES & LENORA HUETT

THE AMNESIA FACTOR

CELESTIAL ARTS
MILLBRAE, CALIFORNIA

First Printing, October, 1975

Made in the United States of America

Library of Congress Cataloging in Publication Data

Mathes, Joseph H   1928–
       The amnesia factor.

       Includes index.
       1. Thought-transference. 2. Interstellar communication.
3. Life on other planets.
I. Huett, Lenora, 1923–   joint author.
II. Title.
BF1999.M437   133.9'3   75–9446
ISBN 0–89087–023–3

*

DEDICATION
To Harold and Herod
the true authors of this book,
who opened doorways to hidden knowledge
with such unique and memorable statements as:

To us, even your instantaneous is slow.

* * *

Acknowledgment

Perhaps more appropriate than attempting individual acknowledgments, would be a sincere expression of deep gratitude to all who contributed, down through the ages, to man's massive pyramid of knowledge; to those who, despite quicksands of time and human nature, forged out into new territory to expand the frontiers of human advancement. A special depth of gratitude goes to one in our midst who has selflessly devoted his life to this very cause. Departing the serenity of homeland and friends to aid a turbulent, frenetic Western society, he arrived seemingly empty-handed. But the *gift* he brought so gently across the oceans has enriched and uplifted the lives of more than 500,000 Americans in all walks of life. Available to everyone, this effortless technique for achieving deep, blissful rest twice each day produces an amazing range of cumulative benefits. It is natural, positive, and progressive in its improvements to human systems. Business, education, health, and government are enthusiastically endorsing this scientific, extensively researched preparation for activity and creativity. In addition to his ceaseless direction of a World Plan Movement, the expansion of many centers, and opening universities in seventeen countries, he has taken time to author the exquisite new *Commentaries on the Bhagavad Gita,* correcting many centuries of misinterpretation. On behalf of 8000 teachers of his unique gift, the students at MIU, and all TM'ers worldwide, we convey our deepest appreciation to this paragon of peace and lover of humanity, Maharishi Mahesh Yogi; and to his beloved Teacher: Jai Guru Dev eternally.

CONTENTS

Introduction

Whose child has never wondered, "What am I?" and what philosopher has not pondered the questions, "What am I for?" and even more profoundly, "Why?"? Our ancestors gazed in wonder at the same clusters of stars and constellations in the heavens as do today's astronomers, and the same question continues to tantalize interested minds: "Might there be someone else out there?"

There are answers to these questions, answers that have long been obscured by veils of misinterpretation. Today, space technology is extending the vision of human eyes far beyond the borders of our solar system, out beyond our galaxy. We have learned that the endless deeps of space contain countless other wheeling galaxies, perhaps other universes. Many large radio-telescopes are continuously listening and probing for intelligent signals from outer space, from an advanced culture "outside." And these highly technical endeavors are not without concrete feedback. Considerable evidence has been collected and analyzed to prove that precursors to amino acids—basic building blocks of living forms—are found in particles recovered from

1

certain space probes, and meteorites have been found which contain ingredients necessary to support life. Such data has been programmed into specialized computers. To the question of whether other life might exist in the universe, these computers have answered in the affirmative. For several years they have shown the mathematical odds to be more than a *million-to-one* that, in our galaxy alone, extensive life *does* exist out there.

Scientists are well aware that even should they overhear an intelligent signal from a faraway culture, the time limitation would effectively prevent trans-space correspondence. Our next nearest star-sun is about 4.3 light-years distant and, with present methods, more than 8.6 long years would creep by, (under the best of conditions), before receiving an answer to our . . . well, what would break the ice? "Hello out there . . . How's it going with you folks?"

This time barrier stems from one basic problem. So far, there has been discovered only one medium through which to transmit radio signals. This is the well-known electromagnetic spectrum. All frequencies pulsing through this ocean move at the speed of light, no faster. This mode may serve well over short distances on earth—even planet to moon—but time lag difficulties increase as the distance increases between planets. Radio control of landing modules and space probes sent to explore distant planets is considered a major problem. (During the many minutes of time lag between transmissions, a robot vehicle might easily wander over the nearest cliff.)

Today, however, a new and better method of communicating is dawning on the horizon of expanding technology. When a machine cannot perform the task, man himself must often substitute. It may be news to some readers that certain high ranking research institutes have probed and examined another spectrum, a completely *different* method of communicating. The *San Francisco Chronicle* of October 23, 1974, under a page 6 headline by Kevin Leary, stated: "*SRI Scientists' Fiindings: A Mysterious Mental Power;* two scientists from Stanford Research Institute have published evidence that they say strongly suggests many persons may have the ability to send and receive information through a strange and as yet unexplained power. The two

SRI physicists published their findings in the [then] current issue of *Nature*, a prestigious top ranking British scientific journal. They stated the phenomenon they had studied for more than a year was not ESP, but something that depended on an unknown, seldom exercised sensory capability possessed by many, perhaps all persons."

This finding seems quite timely and potentially useful, since intricate examination suggests this new method *exceeds* the speed of light. It appears to be instantaneous, and distance seems to be no barrier. One astronaut is reported to have experimented with it while standing on the moon. Some evidence indicates this mode has been long recognized. References are to be found in literature and art, such as Australian aboriginal art which rather pointedly describes the feat of "talking on the wind" to others in faraway lands.

This mode of communications has already been given a name: "*channeling*," and those persons who have developed the ability to transmit and receive other's telepathic communications are called "*channels.*"

To the question, "Why can't everyone channel?" there is evidence that deepseated stresses, beliefs, or hang-ups may completely block the subtle flow of mental information necessary to telepathy. And many of today's channels remain unaware that their own psychological life-conditioning tends to color the delicate translation of those language symbols received. Lenora, the channel in this book (and its co-author), is rated 'superior.' Communications received through her talent have been recently published in *Path To Illumination*, which received enthusiastic acclaim. Lenora is a charming mother of four young adults. She and her husband, Chuck, reside in the San Francisco Bay Area. Chuck is a lean and easy-going type, affable and friendly to all, and completely undisturbed by Lenora's unique talent. This latter blossomed over a period of years to its present fluid state. She has been interviewed by the media and examined by members of the local scientific community. Her one desire seems to be that of helping humanity understand the significance of these expanding times, that *now* is the time to broaden one's outlook and search more deeply.

Lenora's working partner in this book is Joseph H. Mathes, a long-time researcher into origins of life, purposes of creation, and possible visits to this planet by nonterrestrials. Despite volumes of evidence, he maintained a firm, skeptical stance throughout three decades concerning ESP phenomena. But one sunny afternoon in 1971, he was introduced to Lenora by one of his associates who had been working with her for a period of years.

What a jolt that introduction proved to be! Within ten short minutes with Lenora, his limited opinions had to be radically revised. He quickly determined that her telepathic ability was genuine by asking complex questions clearly beyond her field of knowledge. Lenora dazedly stated that she could hardly comprehend the questions, let alone any possible answers, yet the information she channeled was precisely correct. Surprised, he then began to ask questions about subjects beyond his own limited knowledge, and it was at this point that all the fun started.

'Tis easy enough to settle down in one's snug, favorite chair, pick up a book and commence to read, to sail forth upon unknown adventures in the warm security and privacy of one's home. But how rarely are thoughts given to the long hours, the months of creative effort spent composing and collating serial events into a flowing, enjoyable manuscript? Even rarer is a thought given to the intricate tasks handled by the publishing staff. Beyond this, almost nonexistent is the thought that the authors might have had real doubts as to the advisability of publishing their findings during this century.

Such was the case with this book. Its contents are somewhat more than just thought provoking. To those personally present during the portrayed events, the communications and related happenings were rather electrifying. Indecision stemmed primarily from the probability that by publishing these findings at this time, many cherished beliefs might require reexamination. Then, after considerable thought and many discussions, it was felt that the gains outweighed the losses, that the contents of these communiques would surely add considerable cheer and comfort to millions of anxious people, those so deeply in need of a helpful boost in these troubled times. Indepth examination of the scales of the present revealed nothing but imbalance.

But how might one balance the scales of the future? Who among us can say today whether future historians, (assuming there will be any), will praise or condemn a twentieth century decision to explode a myth and open the drapes hiding a window to tomorrow? Will this vista of tomorrow blaze too brightly and dazzle eyes more comfortable behind dark glasses? Such an intrusion could hardly be condoned. A compromise was finally reached with the suggestion that certain of these communications be withheld for a future publication. The major bulk of the transcriptions from the original sixteen tapes are included in this book, which will allow the reader ample opportunity to evaluate the quality, flavor, and value of this information.

What is seen through a window to tomorrow? A vast desolate waste? Or is it a sparkling scene of frolicking children, laughing and playing amidst trees, butterflies, and dappled wildflowers in enchanted glades reminiscent of Tolkien's *Lochlorien*? Perhaps there are those who feel such a paradise is no longer attainable. Those who read this book may find a way, one which is said to be effortless.

Such a fulfilled life, however, cannot come without change. A river's journey is constant change and we who dwell in time's river must discover an easy method of adapting to time's cyclical changes. To remain anchored to the past is to sit like a boulder in the middle of a river. In time, such rocks are worn away, no longer serving as obstacles to an onward progressing, ever creative humanity. It is the very nature of the human mind to seek greater happiness and fulfillment. Even as plants reach toward the life-sustaining rays of the sun, so people reach for greater happiness, security, better times.

But what of those who equate happiness and security with traditional values of the past? Have they not the right to pursue happiness on their own terms, unmolested by the eagerness of others who welcome change and acceleration towards the future? Or is it just possible that some common denominator exists that, if found, might enable both to live happily in peace and harmony? Needless to say, had not this underlying factor been found, this book would never have reached the publishers. As parents, the authors could never sanction the addition of further anxieties to an already overstressed society. Rather, it is expected that these findings will, in time, help alleviate many of our twentieth century fears and limitations.

And perhaps a word of caution will lessen future frictions resulting from those who allow their emotions to affect their common sense. Need it be stated that we're all in this together, that we all inhabit the same planet? And that our planet is, in truth, a "ship" in outer space?

The Amnesia Factor is the result of a series of tape recorded events during 1971–72, adventures in a new field of communications which led to a discovery, a deeply hidden planetary secret. This finding may help explain not only the strange history of humankind but the fundamental purpose of human existence. It is the "Why?" of creation and planetary progress, the essential *meaning* of human struggles, that baffles the intellect. The authors feel that were it not for this new method of communicating, without the kind understanding and reciprocity of those "outside," these revealing insights might well have remained unknowns until future times. While regarded as personal discoveries, both writers are well aware of the saying: "There is nothing new under the sun." It is also true that certain historic writings seem to parallel several of the findings, which is not unusual. But how rare it is to be privileged to probe *behind* the triple veils of symbolism, far deeper than surface knowledge, and search along unknown paths toward the deepest secret of all.

There is no book, however massive or enlightened, which contains *all* answers to an infinite creation, yet it will be found that two small letters of the alphabet can open a doorway to limitless discoveries. There may yet be many adventures ahead for humanity, not only on this small planet but perhaps in countless other systems; and it might prove beneficial, before commencing a journey through unknown territory, to learn that a destination truly exists.

For all who seek fresh adventures, for those who still delight in unique treasure hunts, and for those who enjoy meeting the unknown and unexpected, it is hoped that this book will serve as a satisfying introduction to those "outside."

Prologue
Amnesia Island (Fable)

Long, long ago, in a timeless kingdom of surpassing beauty and
harmony, dwelt a great and wise King. Most of His Majesty's
royal children had earned their inheritances, had long since
begun to rule over their own lesser realms. But two royal children
yet remained, growing in the love and warmth of their Father's
castle. And when they had reached a certain age, the King then
decreed that they should go forth and meet the Seven Challenges,
from which they would gain the strength, wisdom, and compassion so necessary to those who would rule kingdoms of their own.

Six times, the prince and princess were disguised and secretly
sent forth to live and work amongst six different peoples of six
different trades. And six times, these royal children returned to
their Father stronger, wiser, and with deeper compassion for
those who served the kingdom.

Then the seventh and final Challenge was faced. The two children must descend into the very depths of the realm, to live and
toil in the lowermost level of Nature's workshop, to develop a
lasting appreciation for Nature's creative experiments. Here, for
the very first time, they would encounter "change," constant and
ever-present cycles of seasons and changing conditions, as well as

*the waves of opposites: pleasure and pain, love and hate, ease
and hardship. Change, they were to discover, was itself the hidden law behind creativity. Thus the King had decreed that, above
all, His children must learn well the lessons of adapting to
change.*

*But as the King looked upon His young and still innocent chil-
dren, His heart began to melt. With great love and mercy, He decided to shorten the seventh and final Challenge by granting
them temporary "forgetfulness." Without their memories, the
royal children would not suffer from remembrance of their
golden years in the castle. Rather, they would set forth with fresh
eagerness to learn their lessons.*

*When the children heard this, they immediately asked their
Father how they could ever find their way home without
memories. The King laughed and replied that when the final
Challenge was completed, He would send a royal messenger to
fetch them. But again they hesitated, knowing that without
memories, they might not believe the messenger. And the King
again replied that, in this case, He would simply send more royal
messengers until they believed. And if none were believed, He
would then send one of their elder brothers, a royal Prince, to
fetch them.*

*Greatly reassured, the young prince and princess then donned
their new disguises and, when all preparations had been made,
drank the magic potion of forgetfulness. When they had fallen
asleep, they were gently borne to Nature's experimental isle,
(which is known to this very day as Amnesia Island) to commence
the Seventh Challenge.*

*But there was one secret the King never revealed to them. He
so dearly loved His precious children that He could not bear the
thought of them alone and memoryless, wandering as naked
babes in Nature's forests. So He sent His most trusted and beloved Guardians to watch over them wherever they roamed.*

THE
AMNESIA
FACTOR

Chapter 1

Space Missions

Lenora sat very quietly beside me as we drove toward my home. The late evening twilight seemed electrically charged, and she seemed nervous. I felt a twinge of regret that, by my invitation, Lenora would be exposed to a battery of questions on subjects she knew nothing about.

We were on our way to meet three of my friends, Ken, Paul, and Dwight, who shared with me a common interest in science, particularly in the investigation of UFO (Unidentified Flying Object) sightings.

Arriving, I introduced Lenora and drew the drapes, enclosing the five of us in seclusion and comfort. Coffee was served as the tape recorders and projection screen were set up. We soon discovered that Lenora knew nothing about UFOs, nor did she have any real interest in such things. Paul then began projecting slides onto the screen. As a test, he asked Lenora if the UFO in the picture was real or fake. Gradually overcoming her shyness, Lenora faintly murmured, "That one feels like a fake." Then another UFO flashed onto the screen and she hesitated, looking far away. Suddenly she stated, "That's the real thing." Then another lighted the screen. Leaning forward, she stated, "That, too, is a real object. I can sense that there was life on board that craft." We stared at Lenora. Somehow, I could tell that she had been accurate. As the slide show continued, Lenora kept her answers brief but gradually became more interested and sure of herself.

Ken suddenly asked, "Lenora, how are you determining the validity of these slides? How do you do it?" She smiled and replied, "Mostly it's a matter of feel, or thought-sensing. I get impressions of either a hoax or a real UFO craft. And also, *they* can help by advising me."

This changed the tone of the session, since the trio had to know who *they* were, and how *they* could be so accurate in their evaluations. Lenora told us that there were those on the "other side," more specifically, those who were knowledgeable about UFOs, who were telepathically aiding her.

We exchanged glances. Clearly this was going to become an even more interesting evening than we had anticipated. Continuing to project slides, Paul lapsed into his lecture format by stating the circumstances surrounding each sighting.

"This photograph was taken by a scientist—Ph.D. in chemistry—who was on vacation in Oregon at the time. He spotted this UFO rising from behind a low hill. The odd part is that his camera was later checked and found to be all right, but the photo clearly shows the UFO fading away! We'd like to find out if UFOs are able to penetrate into dimensions other than ours."

Lenora leaned back, closed her eyes very briefly, then surprised us all by rattling forth the following strange message:

━━━━━

They could, but do not. Their vibrations vary within the bounds of those energy layers within the physical matrix. They are able to reach a different vibration, yet are still here.

━━━━━

Considerable discussion then followed. Ken spoke of phase transitions in the field of subatomic particles, such as tachyons. These particles, of incredibly tiny mass, were calculated to be of variable velocity, moving at various speeds at superlight velocities. Physics, he stated, was attempting to formulate a theory that could accommodate particle behavior which seemingly transcended Einstein's theory of relativity. His point was that a UFO craft utilized by an advanced culture, a spacecraft capable of traversing the great distances between solar systems, would very likely be constructed of a type of material such that its mass could be converted. Without this variable, the fixed mass of a spaceship would be restricted to sublight velocities.

Dwight mentioned that whatever this "tachyon theory" turned out to be, it might provide a solution to the puzzle of how UFOs reach our planet from far distant star systems. Then other scientific possibilities were discussed.

Dwight looked thoughtfully at Lenora. "Have you ever heard of the Bow and Arrow case?"

"No, I haven't," she slowly replied.

He briefly described the incident that had happened in the fall of 1964 to three young men, bow hunters, up in the Sierra Nevadas near Cisco Grove. While hunting, they had become separated near dark. Two of them returned to their campsite and the third elected to spend the night on a ridge. The next morning, the straggler stumbled into camp with quite a wild tale. His friends had considerable difficulty getting him to calm down. He was still trembling.

Settling down for the night, he stated, he'd observed a light moving from the horizon toward his position. Thinking it might be a rescue helicopter, he'd quickly started three small signal fires about ten feet apart. The light came close, hovered over his head, but to his amazement, it made no sound at all! Sensing something alien, he'd instantly climbed the nearest pine tree and hid. Shortly thereafter he'd seen a lighted module flash vertically down from a back-lit, rectangular portal in the underside of the UFO craft, and soon heard the sounds of someone moving through the brush toward his position. A short time later, two 'robots' and two smallish humanoid beings came up to his tree. They made no sound. Panicked, feeling threatened, the lad had cocked a steel-tipped hunting arrow in his bow and fired it point blank at one of the robots. It hit the robot in the chest area and, with a shower of sparks, it merely glanced off. Twice more he fired, but the arrows only shoved the robot back slightly. The small humanoids just stood in the background, quietly observing. But when they finally tried to boost each other up into the tree, the tense hunter struck matches to his oil-soaked hat and tossed the flaming torch down at them. This caused them to retreat rapidly. After a sudden gesture from one of the humanoids, the robots emitted a whiff of gas into the tree, causing the lad to pass out. Fortunately, he had wisely fastened his belt around a branch and this precaution saved him from falling out of the tree.

When he regained consciousness, the charade continued for hours and hours. He threw nearly everything in his possession down at them, even his shoes. Finally, both robots faced each other at close range and a sudden exchange of bright flashes between them produced a large cloud of gas. Again, the hunter passed out. When he awakened, the sun was dawning and the visitors were nowhere to be seen.

In camp, he'd insisted to his hunting buddies that these beings could not have been human because they didn't know how to get him out of the tree. Any human person could have easily accomplished this by several well-known means.

Dwight then asked Lenora what the motive behind such a contact might have been. Again Lenora briefly closed her eyes, then looked at us and pronounced:

▬▬◆◆◆◆

These crew members had never before encountered fear-vibrations. They were fascinated by the radiations emanating from the one in the tree. They meant no harm, merely stimulated the outpouring vibrations.

◆◆◆◆▬▬

Lenora seemed rather surprised that the answers coming through her were generating such debate among the rest of us. (None of us, at that time, knew that oftentimes a channel cannot recall answers that flicker through the mind at high speed. Lenora simply couldn't remember what she'd said and was too polite to mention it. She listened to our discussions and learned from these what her answers had revealed.) The impact of this most recent answer caused us to wonder aloud what kind of culture, what type of civilization could produce people who were unacquainted with fear-vibrations? Could other areas of our galaxy be so far in advance of our planet's culture that their citizens had matured beyond fear? Ken pointed to the present-day knowledge that galaxies develop from the center outwards, so it would seem logical that the older cultures would be found nearer the center of the Milky Way. They would have a considerable time-jump on our planet, which is out in the fringe area. Dwight continued by asking Lenora what the purpose of the Bow and Arrow UFO craft might have been. Why was it in that particular area of the Sierra Nevadas?

When she closed her eyes this time, a lengthy pause ensued. Suddenly a completely different style of voice, one of commanding authority, answered:

▬▬▬▬▬

This craft in no way belonged to squadrons under specific orders to watchguard the planet. It is not of that order, but of a smaller group that flits among planetary systems eagerly searching for a type of isotope useful in their metallurgy. This was the prime reason for their presence in that mountainous area on that night in 1964. We extend our personal apology. In no way was this craft ordered or allowed near the surface of this planet. Their foolishness in seeming attack has caused much furor and is not to our liking. Please extend sympathy to him who received ill treatment. They should have known better. It is a pity that their training was inadequate. They did not recognize simple emotion on the vibrational scale. It was a lack of training. These ones are not emotionless, but nearly so. They are not aggressive, merely overly curious, as a scout such as Magellan or Cook. They stumbled into a situation beyond their understanding. No harm was meant.

▬▬▬▬▬

It would be difficult to attempt to describe the intense feelings that surged through us at that moment. We all experienced a sense of excitement about the importance of what was happening before our very eyes.

Lenora was then asked if these UFO crewmen were telepathic:

Almost completely. These are rather unemotional, more scientific.

━━ ━━ ━━ ━━ ━━

Ken then asked about the intent of UFO activity over the past decades:

━━ ━━ ━━ ━━ ━━

There are those who are just watching, such as a watchdog would watch over his particular charges. These are the ones who are greatly concerned over those matters that are going on, on the earth at this time, those who are well aware of the thought-forms that are coming forth, well aware of the emotional upheaval, those who are concerned only with keeping the balance, that this particular planet not set off a chain reaction that could be devastating to other areas of the universe. These are the minor part of those who are watching. There are also those who are attempting to establish contact, or to be able to deliver information which could be helpful to the earth people. The intent of 95 percent of these is of a peaceful, helpful, knowledgeable purpose, and yet man must constantly use his own vigilance, his own thinking, his own intuition as to the way in which he should make contact. Caution is always a key word. Above all things, move slowly.

━━ ━━ ━━ ━━ ━━

Thinking about the 5 percent who were less than constructive, the question was asked, "Is there any way to differentiate between these categories?"

━━ ━━ ━━ ━━ ━━

There is no insignia on these, but three points could be made: one, telepathy; two, intuition; three, none of these are overly aggressive. This means 100 percent. There is no harm of this nature. Our pilots are not responsible for side effects, burns, scars, etcetera, since they are ordered not to linger on the surface, due to the emotional upheaval on the planet. Their contacts are of an essential, confidential nature.

━━ ━━ ━━ ━━ ━━

Question: "What are UFOs, and from where do they originate?"

These are valid, material ships, or flights, as earth would call them, from other areas of the universe. They are for the most part from within your own galaxy. There is a need here to make a valid contact. This has been done in the past and will be done in the future. This has been done for longer than the memory of those who are present in this room. This has been going on for many centuries, and it is not new to these particular crewmen. They have come before, they will come again. They have been rejected many times, and yet they have been accepted many times. There has also been the worship of these particular ones, and this is not something which they desire. There is an earnest desire to work in cooperation with those of the earth, and though the need is not there to share information, it is there to be able to establish new ports, or contacts.

━━━━━

Question: "Are some of the Biblical descriptions of lights in the sky actually attributable to UFO spacecraft as we know them today?"

━━━━━

Yes.

━━━━━

Question: "And is this where the worship comes in, that you speak of? Perhaps establishing them as gods?"

━━━━━

Yes. There was a total lack of understanding, and yet those who came down were of good report—were doing a worthwhile service, were giving beneficial information—and thus those of the earth knew that this was something which could be looked up to, or worshipped. The contact was beneficial.

━━━━━

When questions concerning the propulsion techniques of these UFO craft were raised, Lenora looked embarrassed. She said they were telling her that she did not contain within her memory banks sufficient terminology to describe it. She relayed their statement that crystals were involved, also complex magnetic fields of an ultrahigh frequency nature. Physical propulsion methods were not needed; other sources of energy were used.

When the subject of the Bermuda Triangle came up, the question was asked if any of the many disappearances of ships were caused by UFOs:

━━●━●━●━━

No. There is a 'fault' in the universe that causes this. The planet lies in the path of several powerful energy streams . . . These are not easy to control. However, know that the best possible is being done at all times.

━━●━●━●━━

Lenora said she was being shown a powerful and tightly defined "suction area," that the convergence of the planet with these streams of energy sometimes formed a vortex which swept up the ships and aircraft into space.

Then the subject of UFO crewmembers who have occasionally interviewed human beings (such as Betty and Barney Hill), then "memory-erased" them, was discussed. Ken asked, "Hypnosis has revealed that these people were taken aboard UFO craft and interviewed, but their memories were erased beore they were released. Why do the UFO crewmembers want these contacts unrevealed?"

━━●━●━●━━

Ridicule is so prevalent that this is being done for the safety of those who have been participants. It is also well that this has happened, for it would cause them undue pressure from within—extreme pressure in fact—if they were to recall readily those things which had happened. There was no harm which occurred, and yet the experience is so real and so valid. This would be totally doubted by those with whom they come in daily contact. No, it is necessary that this (memory erasing) be done so that they can be at ease with themselves.

━━●━●━●━━

The next series of questions concerned a number of "disappearances," case reports of men who had simply vanished. Lenora explained each one of these; most were due to natural causes. A more interesting case concerned two highly educated scientists who had disappeared. Lenora answered that these two had willingly gone with a UFO spacecraft, that they were even then being of considerable help to scientists in another system, and by no means did they desire to return to this planet.

Then an odd thing happened, or did not happen! One of the group asked about the two moons of Mars, whether one of them might be "artificial." Lenora simply could not get an answer! They waited patiently, but nothing came through. Lenora began apologizing, but the whole group reassured her that such information might be "classified." Perhaps these two moons were destined to play a part in man's future space explorations, and the most tactful manner of handling a premature question would be to say nothing.

Sensing the approach of the meeting's end, I asked, "In the final analysis, does humanity have anything whatsoever to fear from UFO craft?"

No. Most of these spacecraft are on benevolent missions, such as observation, or surveillance, or contacts. We repeat, these must not be feared.

Paul had one final question. "We've received reports that the astronauts on the Apollo 12 moon mission radioed back that they were observing flashing lights both ahead of and behind them. Were they being "escorted," and why?"

Yes. This was to protect them from colliding with space debris. Their path was cleared by those convoy craft.

Then, when asked about the relatively short stature of some UFO crewmen, Lenora forwarded the answer that this was due to higher gravity conditions on their home planet.

Then the session broke up and I drove Lenora home. When I sincerely praised her poise and calm in the face of so many questions, she sighed with relief and murmured, "I'm just glad it's over!" Carefully phrasing the question, I then asked, "There are many other facets to this puzzle, Lenora. I've been studying some advanced books that raise many questions. Would it be possible for me to come to your home sometime, just for a private session?" Lenora laughed openly and replied, "Why certainly! I'd be delighted!"

Even after such a remarkable evening as we had experienced, I was not even remotely prepared for what was to come.

Chapter II
Communications with a Legend

"Wonder if I've forgotten anything?" I pondered. I rechecked my supplies, the line cord and mike, the cassette recorder, notebook and pen, the pretty bouquet of flowers, then loaded the pile into my car, Betsy, and warmed up her engine. I reflected that I really knew very little about Lenora. She had four lovely children; her husband was a contractor. I had been advised that her gift of telepathy was not yet widely known.

Arms loaded with supplies, I rang the doorbell and Lenora's warm, cheerful face greeted me. She cordially invited me in and, genuinely delighted with the flowers, disappeared into the kitchen for a vase. I found a handy wallplug for my recorder and was testing the mike when she returned to place the flowers on the dining room table. Flashing a quick smile, she seated herself and began the conversation.

Discussing telepathy, I learned that her abilities had not appeared suddenly; rather, they had emerged from practicing a form of "automatic writing." Lenora had gradually become aware that she could feel the answers to questions even before she wrote them down. She had then been helped by friends to learn to unblock and allow the information to freely flow through her mind and voice. Gradually, over a period of years, this ability became quite fluid. Lenora remains conscious at all times.

"Now, what would you like to ask?", Lenora commenced. Starting up my tape recorder, I mentioned the date: "June 25th, 1971," then proceeded to ask my first question, one that pertained to my fifteen-year-old son, Bill. "My son was born with a badly twisted right leg. Despite surgical techniques and considerable therapy, it appears that the leg will never be normal. Was this karma (cause and effect) from a previous life?"

Lenora paused, looked into the far distance, then slowly relayed:

—————

This was not karmic . . . no, this was a physical defect, something that is not to be of great harm to this child. It is something that will cause him to be more slow in outer activities, but only so that he will develop his mental capacities to the greatest possible degree. Books mean a great deal to him . . . . a decathlon athlete in Greece.

—————

Although mere seconds had passed, I felt that time had suddenly stopped in its tracks. It had never occurred to me that Bill might have deliberately chosen a defective physical body so as to be enabled to focus more firmly on mental achievements. This explained many puzzles, why Bill had never once complained about his handicap, had always accepted everything with a cheerful grin. Yet his zeal toward sports had been obvious. Despite his handicap, and thanks to Bob Randall, his farsighted and soft-hearted baseball coach, Bill had been allowed to play in the peewee and minor leagues. What he lacked in one leg was more than compensated for by his zest for the game, his heads-up alertness, and his cheerful acceptance of unequal odds. No one present would ever forget the fantastic feat that Bill had nearly pulled off, one sunny afternoon at the end of the season. Randall's spunky little twelve-year-olds had made the All Stars and were pitted against a red hot team that towered over Bill's. Undaunted, his team played inspired baseball and held the opposition to a tie score midway through the game. When their pitcher began to tire, Bill came in with an inspired curve-ball and nearly pitched his team to victory. Spectators had gone wild, rooting for the underdogs as they are prone to do, and despite losing the game, everyone went home with ecstatic memories. I could still remember Bill skipping from base to base, yelling encouragement to his team-mates . . . "C'mon Rudy! You can do it! . . . Hit one out of the park!"

It was also easy to recall Bill's eagerness with books and magazines. He'd been especially interested in technical specifications. Having once become dissatisfied with the performance of his little Honda motorcycle, and despite my skepticism, Bill purchased certain technical parts with his own money, installed them himself and proceeded to demonstrate. I remembered the mild shock (and the black tire mark up the street) when I'd learned that Bill could put his money where his mind was and make it pay real dividends!

Turning to my notes, distillations from decades of reading and studying, I asked, "What can I learn about my prior lives? I'm especially interested in Biblical times."

Lenora paused, as if she might be intently "listening." When she spoke, her voice came through almost as if she were reading from some "record":

━━◆━━◆━━◆━━

Tibet . . . a Tibetan monk, one who was greatly interested in herbs and their effects upon other people; interested in the medicinal side of life, although not greatly involved in health problems. On the positive side, one who could see the causes and effects.

━━◆━━◆━━◆━━

Intrigued, I asked her for the name of the monk. Lenora admitted some reluctance with "names." This was her only hangup, but she gamely agreed to try. Pausing, she closed her eyes and slowly spelled out: "T-W-Z-E-N . . . I've never heard of such a name, and I wouldn't even begin to know how to pronounce it!"

With the spelling of the name Twzen, I felt a strange glow flood through my body. I sensed that somehow, in some way, Lenora was quite accurate. She continued slowly, "That felt male, and I also get a male life in Germany. Chemicals seem to be extremely important. I get 'scientist' somewhere in the seventeenth century; the name . . . 'Guggenheim.' It's strange, though, that both these lives seem 'singular.' You don't seem to be working with a group of people or in a large lab. It feels more like 'by myself,' or 'on my own' . . . and research, or a desire to help mankind or those nearby. I don't feel 'high note' or extremely well-known, but known in your field and people are referred to you because of what you have accomplished. You made some kind of a breakthrough at that time."

Again I felt that same strange glow surge through my body when the name Guggenheim was pronounced. Suddenly Lenora continued, "In Roman days, approximately A.D. 500, again male, I get 'lawyer' . . . defense law, or defending the underdog, yet it feels like people of money. This again seems to be that mind of yours that digs into the finite bits and pieces, similar to chemistry and herbs. You find the small detail that's important, especially in law." After a short pause, "Near Biblical times, again I get Roman, but this time it's as an artisan, a worker in silver and jewelry, a male of the working class. You hear of Christianity, but at a distance. No sides are taken. You hear of it and wonder."

This rang a bell. I'd always remained wide open where religions were concerned, preferring to find my own manner of searching. I felt that if I failed, no one else could be blamed, but if I succeeded, I'd have all the pleasure of the quest.

I felt a sudden impulse to ask where this information on my past lives was coming from. That little impulse changed my life.

"Where is this information coming from, Lenora?" She replied that the *Akashic Records* contained all the data on all lives, and that one's "guides" were the guardians of the records. She added that many, many times the guides had withheld information about certain lives because of the scars and trauma connected with them. It seemed to her that a 'blind' covered those particular "windows."

I asked, "Does everyone have guides?"

Lenora hesitated, then shrugged her shoulders, "I should think so."

Curious, I decided to try once again: "Do you suppose you could get me their names?"

Lenora's scowl rather clearly expressed her true feelings about searching for "names." (Much later, I discovered that the cause of her hang-up was bound up in the past. Lenora had innocently told some close friends of her newfound ability with telepathy and, when they tested her by requesting the names of former relatives, she had misspelled a few. Her close "friends" had promptly called her a fake. Such mistreatment had caused Lenora no end of confusion and hurt.)

Lenora commenced, "Now let's see. Where most people feel like they have one guide, with several others in the background, you feel like you have two strong guides with you. One is business or occupation-oriented, the other feels spiritual, and they feel almost equal claim on you. They feel almost as twins. There is no pushing or animosity, such as 'let me in first,' or 'he needs this first.' It's such a very divided, equal feeling, very balanced. They both feel male, or masculine, quite aggressive and strong, but in no way pushy or overbearing." She paused reflectively, then said:

"Well, I get Harold and Herod. Now, you might think Herod relates to King Herod, but it doesn't have any connotation of that. It's just Harold and Herod, and they seem very similar."

With mixed feelings, I asked if perhaps she could get any sort of message from my guides. As if she did this every day of her life, Lenora quickly receded, tuned to a faraway level, and the following words came slowly. There was a marked change in her delivery, as if someone were speaking "through" her from a distance. Her voice quality was very soft:

●━●━●━●━●

Not at this time . . . you are following all the guidance that comes your way . . . you have a very open mind . . . one who listens . . . one who is willing to learn . . . you are not one who looks down on, or derides other people because of seeming stupidity in their actions . . . you overlook the outward appearance and look to the underlying cause . . . you are very understanding, compassionate . . .

●━●━●━●━●

These phrases had a calming effect. The words had a "classic" intonation, totally different from Lenora's usual speech patterns. For the first time, I began to realize the reality of what was taking place in front of my eyes. If, through Lenora's abilities, I could communicate with intelligences in some other dimension, there were a few essential questions that were begging for answers. I had read many works telling of those who had reached Unity and achieved immortality, such as Christ and Buddha, but what was the fate of those less gifted? Carefully framing the question, I asked, "Is there a place for one who has not achieved Unity to serve after this life, if one earnestly desires to serve others?"

There is always a need and a desire on the part of the ALL for anyone who is willing to work. Yes, there is a place for all souls. There is nothing that is wasted within the universe, or outside the universe. All things are put to a purpose and a meaningful existence. Desire is the greatest motivating factor that there is. Whether the soul desires to help or to lack in growth, these are the things that are answered in the beyond. Perfection as you know it now is not a complete state, but only that which will cause you to be sent on to other realms, for what appears to be perfect here is yet imperfect in the higher realms. Know that you must continually seek and continue to grow. This is a part of your desire and your being.

In the silence that followed, in the fading echoes in a room that now felt "open" and multi-dimensional, Lenora asked quietly if the answer had been pertinent to my question. She couldn't recall the context of the answer since it had flowed quickly through her mind. I nodded. Another question stirred in the depths of my consciousness: "Is it proper, in my own personal heart and mind, that I think of God as 'The Divine Architect'? I have a great love of architecture."

You have seen the law and order of the universe, you have seen the beauty and symmetry that is there. You have seen

*this through many, many lifetimes, and it would cause you
to feel that that which has created you would have to be of
an architectural structure or mind. Yes, this is a beautiful
thought and a very complete image of God, for as you take
architecture in its wholeness apart, you will find that each
area is of a complete design and can work within itself. This
is true of the Father, this is true of all parts of His universe.*

━ ━ ━ ━ ━

I finally murmured, "How very, very beautiful. This has been
a truly remarkable experience, Lenora. This could carry me
through the next three lifetimes!" Surprised, Lenora rather
shyly replied, "Well, thank you!"

On July 6th, 1971, I again sat across the table from Lenora,
trying to decide whether the flowers or the hostess beamed the
brightest. Desiring to know more about these "guides," I posed
a direct question, "Where are they?"

━ ━ ━ ━ ━

*We are of a place that is known to you, and yet unknown in
the sense that we can guide and help, but not make things
in your path.*

━ ━ ━ ━ ━

I must have looked puzzled, so Lenora added a further impression: "There seem to be levels or strata where things *can* be
caused to happen physically, but Herod and Harold seem to be
above that level, more of a mental plane."
I continued, "Do you sleep as we do?"

━ ━ ━ ━ ━

*No. We have times of rest from thought, but there is not
the sleeping such as putting one consciousness to the side
and another consciousness taking over. As your unconscious mind continues to work, we continue to work. We
are as that part of you.*

━ ━ ━ ━ ━

"Does it disturb you when I think about you late at night,
when I'm reading or studying?"

No, this is because we have caused you to be aware of us. This is not your thinking, even though you are of this thought.

I asked, "Can you see us as forms?"

We see you as far more than form, because we see the colors, the radiations, the vibrations, the energies that flow forth from you. We see you as "light."

Lenora uttered a startled "Hmm!" at this answer, and my eyebrows shot up. Intuitively, I asked, "In directing questions to either of you, would it help if I vocalized, or could I just think the questions?"

Only in your mind is it necessary. Do not feel overwhelmed by this, do not feel a lack of privacy. We do not judge. The thoughts which you think, and later feel might be of a lesser self, are not unnecessary to you. The thoughts which flow through you are all for your growth. Be aware that they are good at any point, at any rate, and as you think in your heart, so do we hear, and thus we are able to answer. Many of the answers which come to you are not through an actual questioning or conscious thinking on your part, but are because you have unconsciously already asked the questions.

I said, "Well, in that case, they should be aware of my recent studies of *The Urantia Book.*"

Yes. Where do you think this came from? It was planted within the minds of those who are near you, those who have seen your evolvement and, because of this, they were inspired to place this in front of you. None of the things which happen for your growth are happenstance.

I smiled, "Well, I should have guessed that." Then turning a page in my notebook, I asked this: "It is revealed in certain books, such as those by Geoffrey Hodson, that certain basics are desired when contacts such as these take place. First, it is assumed that no individual would hope to personally gain from such contacts; and second, that purity, directness, simplicity and impersonality are desired. Why would 'impersonality' be considered desirable?"

━━━━━

Not being personally involved with any particular one, for through this there is more universality that can be given to all. By a direct contact, there is usually an attachment which eliminates or lessens others. You will find that this impersonality is basically "love," for love is equal to all, and given to all freely. This does not mean a coldness, nor something that is less than personal, but it is not "particular" personal.

━━━━━

I asked, "Why is it that you have volunteered to help humanity progress? Man seems mostly unconcerned with adjacent realms . . . the wild animals in nature, to name one." (The answer came slowly and thoughtfully:)

━━━━━

Do you think any less of the animals of the forest because they do not speak as you do? Do you think less of higher beings that can neither be seen nor heard by those of your realm? . . . (pause) . . . nay, we have love for "all," even as the Father loves all.

━━━━━

Thoughtfully, I asked, "To you, is love not more of a strong affection, rather than the possessive type of love among our kind?"

━━━━━

Love is not necessarily even a physical nor emotional attraction. It can be just a total understanding, a tolerance, a total awareness of the other person and their need. This can be construed as a more expansive love than one has yet learned to give or to receive. Love is a tolerance of all people on all levels. Love is understanding that "right" and "wrong" are only relative, and according to their own particular culture. Love can be affection, but this again is only one facet of love.

━━━━━

Turning another page in my notes, I asked: "If all inhabited creation is 'one vast family,' and God is Father of all and a Father of love, why would He gamble with the lives of some of His children (like us), when even we mortal parents protect our own children?" (An odd thing happened here: Lenora almost jerked and her eyes glazed over. The following answer came through slowly, but with considerable force and power behind it:)

━━━━━━

God does not gamble the lives of His children. He is with them, an essential part and partner with man, throughout all his struggles and adventures on the worlds of time and space.

━━━━━━

We were both startled at the power within this statement, and were to remember the essence of this message later on. I then probed into the question of man's isolation from the rest of the universe.

"Has it not occurred to those in higher levels that a simple monolith of permanent material, suitably engraved with man's true origins and destiny, if placed securely on this planet, might have enabled humanity to evolve more confidently as a brotherhood of common ancestry, more as a friendly family, instead of all the unseen terrors and fears in our past history? If we are created by God the Father, then we truly are His children, and why are we left out here in such isolated, miserable darkness?" (After a pause came this:)

━━━━━━

There was a time . . . when God, in the form of man . . . walked and talked with his brothers and sisters . . . . . these times have been over and over, through the Masters of the past . . . through the times when they walked the earth and tried to describe the supremacy of man over the other areas around him. Man was unable to comprehend. Even though he had seen it in writing, he would not have accepted it as truth. Man has always had the desire to be "less" than one thing and "more" than something else. He has tried to be more than his fellow man, more than his children, and less than a God that he could not see nor fully comprehend. Only by doing this could he rationalize his own movements of being supreme over someone else.

It is necessary that man learn to discipline himself to the extent that he can reach out in love, and not in trembling, to his fellow man; and thus he will be a true son of God, or a son who walks the earth as one who will be fit and able to help populate other planets and systems.

●━━●━━●━━●━━●

I marveled at the sagacity, the wisdom in such a farsighted answer. Then I related to Lenora how I had become inspired one recent evening, during reading, when I discovered that (according to *The Urantia Book*) a group of highly intelligent specialists, dealing exclusively with planetary ecology, had spread out through this sector of space many billions of years ago with the purpose of implanting life on those planets that appeared promising. Selecting this planet for experimental evolution, their work had spanned many millions of years to produce the countless varieties of flora and fauna, first in shallow seas, then on land when the atmosphere was made more hospitable. This planet's close proximity to the sun caused them to erect a protective envelope, (our ionosphere), to screen out much of the sun's ultraviolet radiation. The original plans, though complex, were quite complete; they called for a future ecological balance and harmony in nature. Certain unexpected results backfired, but these retrogressions were the isolated few as compared with the millions of successes.

"Therefore, through you, Lenora, I'd like to read this message to Harold and Herod with the hope that they might somehow transmit it onward." Lenora listened intently and the atmosphere was electric as I read from my notes.

"Kindly transmit my personal and deeply felt gratitude to those scientists, either now resident on this planet or who served here formerly, for their unsung (and mostly unknown), prolonged, yet exquisitely devoted watchcare over the evolutionary ascension of that life which they so carefully placed in our early waters. Be not saddened, nor should you have regrets that your highest hopes were not realized on this planet. It is a source of some comfort to mortal minds that, even to such wise and loyal high beings such as yourselves, plans sometimes do not evolve as expected. Our mortal lives could be much, much worse, and our planet does have many beauty areas, thanks to your efforts. It is hoped that the knowledge gained from those experiments that evolved in our past may augment and uplift the lives of others on other planets of this universe. Others of my kind will come to know and feel elation over your efforts that gave us a life to live. It is also recognized that you have coordinated with many other high beings in your endeavors. One day in the future, my desire is to be permitted to personally embrace you, each and every one of you blessed friends, for your monumental labors on our behalf. Be of good cheer. We are trying to do right, and your hopes and our aspirations will someday be as one in our Father."

Lenora sat still, wide-eyed and astonished, murmuring, "That's beautiful!" Then, unexpectedly, she came to 'attention' and began to speak forcefully, clearly, and with considerable warm emphasis:

━━━━━

This has been a high day. It is well to know that more and more of the earth in this time are recognizing the fact that they are neither new to the cosmos nor on the last legs of their journey. It is necessary that mankind know that this is an ongoing process, that nothing is lost, that time is essential and yet it is not, in that there is eternity and aeons of time to be working.

Man is not on the threshhold of doom, as so many broadcast, but is yet in the darkness of his full day. Know that there is time ahead and much must be accomplished. This is being done. There is new light dawning every day upon the earth, and with this comes new knowledge to other souls. You are living in an exciting time of awakening for the era. Go forth and broadcast as you are able.

━━━━━

Taking a short break after this unusual announcement, we talked of the rapid rise of technology in this century; that transportation had zoomed from horse-drawn buggies to mach-2 jet aircraft; that microwave ovens, color television sets, radar traffic control, communications satellites, and many other unique accomplishments had become everyday realities; and that finally man had achieved the climax of the ages: he stood triumphantly on the moon. At such a time, we agreed it was indeed encouraging to hear that humanity "is not on the threshhold of doom, as so many broadcast."

Resuming the questioning, I learned that Harold and Herod were "high-energy beings," and I decided to probe into their mode of life. I asked, "We re-energize by rest, eating, and drinking. The lack of, or the withholding of any of these essentials, soon kills us. What would be the end result if you, Harold and Herod, did not re-energize?"

━━━━━

Our re-energizing takes the form of "giving." It is a flowing through of energy, by us and through us, that is our reinforcement. We find that as we receive from higher realms, we give to lower realms, and thus we are used as channels. This is our energy-force. (There was a short pause.)

If we were to refuse to give beyond, we would then not be able to receive more, and become static rather than dynamic. It is to our benefit to continue to work. It is also a great joy, and joy becomes light, light becomes energy, around and around we go.

━━━━━

The simplistic beauty of such statements seemed strikingly different. Not the slightest trace of "looking down" at mortals was evident, such as stating something like "We do not die as you do." Rather, their statements seemed positive, tactful, and gracious.

I then turned to the subject of "pain." I tried to portray its burden on humanity, in the physical, emotional, as well as mental areas. When I finished, the following came through at a fast clip:

━━━━━

Man can overcome the pain of body, for this is, though it seems very real to him, something which his intellect or mind can erase or rise above, even as the mystics in the Far East have been able to lie on beds of nails. For this is a part of the body which needs to be controlled or subjugated, even as the animals of the field are subjugated to man. This was given to him as a power from God in the beginning. Remember that those things which cause pain are many times increased through the unconscious memories of past lives, times when man has truly suffered real pain. Now there are many anesthetics, but the pain goes on even though the conscious mind is not aware of it. Thus man can learn to anesthetize himself against these things and become the living soul that he is. The anticipation of pain is only because man desires to draw back from that which he needs to face. If he can face it, he will many times find that the pain is not actually as extreme nor as difficult as he would have imagined. Imagination is a God-given talent, or gift, and through the imagination, one can imagine that he is not suffering pain, or is not an eternal part of it, that this too shall pass away. He will be able to learn to control these things through his mind, with his mind, and in such a manner as to still protect himself against the thing which causes pain. For instance, if it is a disease, he will be aware enough of this to be able to seek medical attention, and yet able to block from himself those things which cause him the emotional stress and strain, for the emotional pain is far deeper than physical pain.

━━━━━

As Lenora—remembering parts of this answer—commented on its contents, I thought it through and decided to privately experiment with pain control. Then I continued, "I'm curious. Does your memory-recall *vary*, or is it inherently *total* among those of your kind?"

━━━━━

It varies according to the need. There are those who have the need to seek the past and its problems so that they will be better able to adjust to their own present life, and for these, they are able to recall. Those who have no need to recall will not be given the facility or faculty of doing this.

Under proper conditions, it is possible for all to have total recall. However, remember that this would be as . . . that one . . . viewed it at the time. It will not be a dispassionate viewing.

━ ━ ━ ━ ━

"Sounds like it's on a need to know basis," I said. "Very efficient, really. I wonder what they might say about sun energies? Just how do mortals benefit from the sun's radiations?"

━ ━ ━ ━ ━

There are very beneficial rays . . . also a degree of warmth that is necessary to the human . . . there is the receiving of certain vitamins and energies that are absorbed . . .

━ ━ ━ ━ ━

Lenora suddenly stopped the answer to remark that they were "showing" her a person without sunlight being similar to a pale plant without the green; but that even without sunlight, the mind functioned. Then she flicked her eyes and continued with the answer:

━ ━ ━ ━ ━

The mind does not necessarily need sunlight. However, it is most beneficial, for as the body is able to be more vital, so can the bloodcells which feed the mind. The mind is an ongoing part which exists without blood and cells, but the improvement of these clarifies it.

━ ━ ━ ━ ━

Lenora echoed my thoughts with the pointed comment: "Sure sounds like a confirmation of life after death, doesn't it?" I nodded my head, then forced my attention back to the study notes. "There would seem to be many different types of 'high-energy beings' on other levels, or in other dimensions. Does your form contain certain unique capabilities, or do your abilities result from your lengthy training?"

━ ━ ━ ━ ━

No, we inhabit several different forms as the progress moves forward. As one reaches higher levels or planes, there are different forms of expression. Thus one can be recognized without a title or a knowledge, for there is a separate form.

━ ━ ━ ━ ━

"Well, during your training, did you gradually learn to control energies and rays, to transmute them, to mind-create, to travel to and between different planes, and to self-multiply yourselves, or were these and other talents natural to your type of beings?"

▬▬▬▬▬

These were inbred, these were a part of our being. These had been developed through many aeons, before we were created as the seraphim.

▬▬▬▬

I was totally unprepared for this statement. Until that moment, I had theorized that the communications coming through Lenora originated from people in some other plane or dimension; that these were just far more advanced people. Despite numerous books that mentioned the "beings of light," the legendary "shining ones," I had always regarded these angelic symbols as myths, pure mythology. Now I wasn't sure. Perhaps there might be some truth to those ancient accounts. My mind wavered, wondering . . . Could they be pulling my leg? . . . Or could they really be seraphim! As if in direct reply to my unspoken question, the following statement—calm and forthright—came through Lenora quite clearly. My doubts fled on the winds.

▬▬▬▬▬

We are honored by this title.

▬▬▬▬

"So they really do exist!" I exclaimed. Then I asked, "I've been reading about another group, those that are said to live midway between our plane and others. Can you tell us, what is a 'midwayer'?"

▬▬▬▬▬

This is one who is in closer contact with the earth vibrations; one who is able to be the "go-between," the contact-force that can also tune in to much higher planes and be able to interpret or feel the answers so that they can be given into a language that is more understandable to the earthling.

▬▬▬▬▬

Lenora suddenly laughed. "Finally something makes real sense!" she declared. "Every time I've tried to sense these guides directly, all I get are rather exotic musical tones—sort of a musical 'language,' I'd guess. But from that last answer, I can now see that this 'midway group' has been functioning as our "translators," interpreting that musical language into English, and vice versa. Without them, we'd never understand a word!"

I asked, "If we're on the Third Plane, what plane are the midwayers on?"

Lenora said she was getting: "Seventh through Ninth," so I then asked what plane Harold and Herod were on. "Thirteenth," she said, but added that they seemed to have the ability to penetrate into denser planes, nearer the physical.

"Lenora says she senses a deep compassion, a great depth of understanding in you," I said. "It is difficult to understand how you can even begin to relate to us unless you had once lived as we do, stuck in a physical body."

We have. Were we with you in flesh bodies, we could be good friends.

That same strange glow surged through me again. I glanced at Lenora, wondering if she might be noticing the effect, but she was just patiently smiling, awaiting the next question. "What plane is the 'soul' on?"

It is all-dimensional.

This answer, like so many others, could not be easily understood by either of us. Many months of further sessions, of indepth probing and studying, were to be absorbed before a clear picture could be seen. As the end of the session approached, I asked a vital question, "Did we, our souls, embark upon this type of 'adventure' with a real purpose in mind?"

It was the need for a soul to fully comprehend all of the gamut of experiences that was necessary to make a fully

understanding nature. It was the need to experience emo-
tions on a physical basis as well as emotions on a spiritual
basis. It was the necessity to feel pain, to feel anger, to feel
hurt, to feel love, and love that would be an expectant love,
rather than one that was given selflessly. It was necessary
to experience all these things, that even spirit might more
fully understand those who are in higher forms, near and
around.

It was not total perfection in the beginning, although
man had seen total perfection in that he had seen the ALL.
His soul was able to comprehend that which was expected
of him, and he knew the route that was necessary to go
. . . he knew the lessons that he would have to take, and
yet even then, each soul is an individual; there is not a set
pattern or mold. It was necessary for each to experience in
a different way and in different time segments.

It was not a total desire on the part of all, for many felt
that they had already reached a stage that was well with
them and they desired to go on. These are those who are
reluctant to be on the earth, or to remain there. These are
those who appear to be of another world or in another
thinking, even a good part of their time on earth.

There were those who were anxious to enter this exper-
ience and to feel with all of their being. These are those
who are so enthusiastic about life, those who immerse
themselves in all the situations and "eat it up."

━━━━━

Lenora and I compared the life attitudes and reactions of some
of the different people we had known. I then bid her a warm and
grateful goodbye, assuring her that the information seemed not
only quite valid, but extremely illuminating.

All the way home, Betsy hummed along merrily. So did I.

Chapter III

Experiments with Control

Up in the office, I completed a report and automatically turned to sign up for my next assignment. Pen in hand, I suddenly remembered my hospital appointment. "Say Al, I won't be in, Monday. Taking some sick leave for minor surgery. Call you when I get released. It won't take long, a few days or so." Al replied, "No sweat. I'll cover you."

Greeting Betsy out in the chill darkness of the parking lot, I climbed in and warmed up her engine. Listening to the subtle changes in idle speed as the Weber carburetors warmed, I began to think about the upcoming surgery. "Sure will be nice to get rid of the aches and pains," I thought. "Wish I could think of some way to imagine the pain away . . ."

Once again we deftly slid into the night traffic, heading homeward. As one part of my mind drove a safe distance behind the traffic, another pondered the problem of how to utilize imagination to overcome pain. What I needed was some form of control, some type of mental control. Rather than a fixed image, I instinctively searched for a dynamic or moving image, something I had learned to control. Remembering my flying, I recalled the sound of the engines when the throttles were pulled back. If pain con-

39

trol could be represented by those throttles, perhaps I could diminish real pain by using my imagination to pull them back to idle.

My plans had been carefully laid for admittance to the hospital Monday afternoon. Telling no one, preferring not to trouble my family, I had reserved a private room without television, so as to read and work on my pain experiment in privacy. Then I pushed all such thoughts 'over the dam' and worked up my notes for Monday (July 17, 1971), an early morning session with Lenora.

Arriving promptly at nine, I noticed the medical emblem on the sedan parked in Lenora's driveway. My heart skipped a beat as I wondered if anything had happened to Lenora. "God," I silently prayed, "Don't let this priceless opportunity slip from our grasp now! We've waited so long." Just as I reached the porch area, the front door opened and an armful of tape recording equipment followed by a smiling gentleman exited. I smiled in return, realizing (with relief) that the doctor had been visiting Lenora for the same reason that I was! Lenora's eyes were sparkling a big friendly welcome in the doorway as I gallantly handed her the bouquet of huge pink carnations.

When she returned to the living room with the floral arrangement, we got right down to business. I read a prepared thesis which had been designed to elicit answers. It attempted to portray man as a "robot"—albeit constructed by an intelligence transcendent to man's—a man-robot which would provide growth-data for 'higher research.' My question was, "What is the fate of the man-robot when the research is completed?" (The answer seemed quite serious.)

◆◆◆◆◆

You are placing robots here without the soul-image that is necessary for them to have, to experience the beauty of that creation which has come forth from them. They must have a "soul" before they become a living being or other than of a lower plane . . . even the animals have a soul.

You have given a beautiful simile to things that would seem to reflect a life around you. However, you are well aware that man is not a robot, and though he is made in some likenesses toward the image of his Father-Creator, he is also a separate individual, distinct and apart from that particular being. Know also that even as a metal robot could not begin to evolve and think. . . that this is a God-given "gift" or something which comes from an outside source—such as from Father to son, as God to soul or being—this is an essential part of man upon the earth.

Know that man can become a co-creator with his Father-God, that he can also reach out to other areas of space and yet be a functional human being. Know that even as he grows and expands in his conscious awareness of those gifts that have already been given him, he must continue to become one with the "All," and see all sides to each particular issue that comes up.

▬▬▬▬▬

I had no idea what the "All" was. Hoping to receive the answer to man's eternal question, I asked, "What am I?" (Very slowly came this answer.)

▬▬▬▬▬

You are a part. . of the soul. . that was a part. . of the Creator. You are not. . Total Creator. . but you are an essence. . or droplet. . of that which IS. You are given. . certain rays, or abilities. . to work with. . . certain added gifts and functions. . . and yet these are not a part of your total being. . but they enhance its growth. They are then removed from you. . and you work with other areas. These are not subtracted from. . . but the middle part is removed.

▬▬▬▬▬

I still wasn't satisfied. I could not fathom the phrase, "An essence or droplet of that which IS." What I really wanted to know was whether or not the self-identity of a mortal person could be recovered intact after the death of the physical body. I rephrased the question: "Is that which is recoverable after the death of the physical body, in any other state, in any other dimension, would it be recognizable by me *as me*?"

▬▬▬▬▬

Yes. It has a sense of your feeling, of your worth, of your abilities. It is more than just memory, but also emotion. . . . (there was a pause).

This is the process of growth that has come with you through the many, many aeons. Know that you have a Spark of the Divine that is there. This is with you, whether you recognize it or not. This is not the information that is implanted within you. This is something that you need to seek out, to develop, to realize it is there, before it is yours to use.

◆━━◆━━◆━◆━◆

I suddenly caught the clue, asking, "Is this Divine Spark the same thing as described in Eastern literature as the 'monad,' or is it perhaps what is called the Divine Thought Adjuster?"

◆━━◆━━◆━◆━◆

The Divine Thought Adjuster.

◆━━◆━━◆━◆━◆

Lenora listened intently as I explained the connection. This God-Spark had been described as a living Spark of the Absolute. The ancient Eastern teachings symbolized God Absolute as the Sacred Flame, from which springs countless Divine Sparks of the Same Absolute Energy. It is said that no purer energy exists in all Creation. This Divine Spark has been described as totally impersonal, yet Its yearning love for Its mortal child seems beyond the comprehension of even higher beings. From the Greek *Agape* it is learned that this is a Divine Love that can wait through the long aeons of time, silently awaiting the moment when Its child turns within and discovers Its loving presence. *Agape*, translated literally, describes a love so pure that, "It forever expects nothing, yet eternally hopes for everything." The Bible describes It as ". . . that true Light that lights every man that comes into the world." The *Bhagavad Gita* portrays It as ". . . smaller than the smallest and greater than the greatest," which hints at Its transcendance of the relative time-space dimensions. The Absolute is primal Source, thus Its parent status has caused It to be called the "Father," "Father Spark," or "Father Spirit."

I asked, "Where is this Divine Spark to be found?"

◆━━◆━━◆━◆━◆

Three inches behind your eyes . . . in the center of your mind.

◆━━◆━━◆━◆━◆

Our feelings were indescribable. In the silence, I thought numbly, "Good Lord . . . . No wonder we've misunderstood. All this time He was hidden in the very last place anyone might have thought to look." Aloud, I asked the question, "In addition to this God-Spark, does everyone also have 'guides'?"

━━━━━

Certainly.

━━━━━

Lenora was then asked to name the guides of each member of the Broome family. Richard Broome, a remarkably talented artist, is a personal friend of mine who developed an unusual technique with invisible paints. Under a 'black-light,' his paintings of aircraft and space scenes magically transform into 'night scenes' of unique realism. I had collaborated with Rick on a "far out" painting which would be unveiled to my family at Christmas. It was during my visit with them that I'd mentioned Lenora and the guides. Rick and Billie, his wife, had become highly intrigued and desired to learn more. I had recommended an excellent book by Jane Roberts, *The Seth Material*, for current information; *The Urantia Book* (no known author) for background and historical details; and *Kingdom of the Shining Ones* for portraits of guides.

At the mention of "names," Lenora looked wary again, much like a spooked and hesitant deer. I coaxed her to try, hoping to help her eliminate the hang-up. Finally she wrinkled her pert nose and settled down to try:

"Well . . . Richard's is Rollo, spelled R-o-l-o-w, and . . . Bethanie . . . I almost get Beth Anne, but it's Bethanie."

"Marsha's is Robert . . . and Michael . . . and there's a third . . . well, it's a very common name . . . Mary . . ."

I was silent, but puzzled over the apparent "slip." Lenora had called Billie, "Marsha." It was six months later when, in a conversation with Rick's mother, I learned that Lenora had been precisely correct! Her nickname was "Billie," but her given name was "Marsha."

I asked if their impish little daughter, Lisa, might have any guides. Lenora closed her eyes briefly to search. "Belinda and

Johnny . . . Belinda and Johnny??? . . . But they feel like *children!* . . . Not at all 'high' or adult! They seem playful!!!" she exclaimed with delight. I was quite surprised. We guessed that little children all over the world very likely had little playmate-companions. Wondering, I then asked, "How do Belinda and Johnny relate to Lisa? Suppose she were to fall while playing in the park and hurt her knee . . . How would they react to this?

◆━◆━◆━◆━◆

They would race off and attempt to attract attention to Lisa, someone who might come to her assistance.

◆━◆━◆━◆━◆

I then asked Lenora (while the iron was hot) if she might get the names of my son's guides. She seemed to be reaching more easily now, and soon said, "This feels female . . . J-o-l-e-n-e . . . Jolene . . . Margaret . . . and Steven. I get two females and a male." I thanked her for the information, then decided to interject some humor into our session. Searching through an old encyclopedia of historical names, I'd stumbled across 'Zuriel.' I asked if Zuriel might still be around, still serving in the same specialized category. Lenora replied that they were giving her a "yes," but, "This one feels 'above' Herod and Harold. . . . Why are you laughing like that?"

I was convulsed and finally got out, "And I know why! Probably just waiting to go to work on the likes of me! Can you guess what that one's specialty is? The encyclopedia stated: 'Zuriel, who holds the cure for stupidity in mankind,' and I couldn't resist asking."

Lenora chuckled, and, as if to prove the point of stupidity in man, the next answer made no immediate sense to either of us. Having worked with high-fidelity music systems for decades, and having a working knowledge of radios and electronics, I knew that transmitters and receivers function more efficiently when "grounded." Likening man's mind to an ultrahigh-frequency transceiver, and recalling that one's nervous system extends down to one's toes, I innocently asked the following question:

"Would standing in water improve man's telepathic abilities?" Lenora's expression reflected amusement as the droll answer came back:

No . . . but sitting in the bathtub might help.

The pretty brunette head with its winged white cap was intently reading a chart on the desk. She made several entries, softly snapped it shut, then returned it to the file cabinet. She glanced at me as I patiently waited beside the counter. "Yes?" she asked, and I gave her my name. She led me down the hallway to the last room on the right and, entering, pulled back the drapes to flood the room with golden sunlight. I noted with satisfaction the sweeping view of parks and green hills beyond the expanse of windows. This side of the hospital faced east.

When the nurse departed, I unpacked my suitcase. Donning slippers and bathrobe, I wandered along the halls, chatted with several patients, then returned to my room. After experimenting with the buttons that controlled the bed adjustment, I curled up and read for several hours. A nurse popped in, apologized for not serving dinner, and briskly filled my water jug. When I growled about not getting fed, she maternally reminded me that I was due in surgery first thing in the morning. Rather magnanimously, I was allowed to drink all the water I wished. Smiling, I returned to my reading.

I was studying a brilliant and high perspective of all the world's best philosophies. A review of history clearly outlined man's long climb from the depths of superstitious fears, through evolving systems of belief that changed with the dawn of each new civilization, each new change a chance to lead humanity toward higher understanding. With the emergence of a true science, and the breakaway from the grip of dominating religions, new potentials for growth arose. I could see that the three giants would eventually merge, forming a more complete "lens" through which to find truth.

"Science, philosophy, and religion," I reflected; "Three different views of the same fundamental Reality. Science probes into Its creative expressions, using limited tools to explore fragments of Its objective manifestations. Philosophy uses the tool of limited mind to try to intellectually probe the meanings, purposes, and values of Its infinite, eternal Mind. Religion attempts to understand It with yet another tool, the heart. And the paradox lies in the futility of trying to describe one's subjective, inner experiences." Just then a young, rather shy little night-nurse entered and asked if I needed a sleeping pill. I declined, saying that I usually read late and slept like a log. And surprisingly, I did.

Somewhat dazed, I awakened in a strange room. One of the nurses crossed the room towards my position, asking, "Awake?. . . . How do you feel?" "Fine," I assured her. "What's your name?" she asked. "It's on my wrist-tag," I reminded her. "No, you tell me," she insisted, so I rather formally recited my name, address, and phone number, then asked the nurse for her's. She chuckled, "You're wide awake, alright." She swung my gurney around, out through the swinging doors into an elevator, and eventually into my room. When I was finally tucked in, I closed my eyes and sighed. Already the ache had intensified, swelling to occasional sharp bursts of needlelike stabbings. I put my imagination to work and visualized my cockpit as vividly as possible. Reaching out with both a mental and physical hand, I slowly pulled back on the imaginary "throttles." No change at all! Grumbling, I tried it again, concentrating all my imaginative powers on the task. Again and again those "throttles" were slowly pulled back and each time I imagined I heard the sound of the engines dying down. No change. I stopped and took a break.

Why would Harold and Herod have stated that pain could be subjugated by the mind's imagination if it were not true? Then a new thought struck; maybe it was simply my small amount of 'mind power' that caused the lack of control. Maybe I didn't have what it takes!

This thought aroused a sort of grim determination and, clenching my teeth, I firmly pulled back on the "throttles" once again. Still no change. Now I began to get angry! There could be no reason for such an inept performance. My imagination was as good as anyone else's! I grumbled, *"Follow* those damn throttles!" and grimly tried it again, and again, and again.

A strange thing happened. I began to notice that although the pain was still there, it now felt "remote." This was all I needed to spur me on. Once again I pulled back on those "throttles," and the pain receded grudgingly. As I refined the technique, I discovered that the clearer I could "see" the cockpit image and the clearer I could "hear" the engines dying down, the sooner the pain subsided. Elated, I practiced every twenty minutes until lunch arrived, then ravenously ate everything put in front of me. Throughout parts of the afternoon, I continued practicing the method and soon achieved a controlling dominance over the postoperative pain.

That evening, some friends dropped in to visit, finding me in a cheerful mood. They were still visiting when the doctor arrived. He recommended that, if I felt up to it, a healing sitz bath might be in order.

Later, I felt strong enough to follow a nurse down the hall to a closetlike room containing the tiniest bathtub I'd ever seen! The nurse checked the water temperature and explained how one backed into a sitting position in the tub. When she departed, I did just that.

Sighing deeply, I leaned back and lit a cigarette, reflecting upon yesterday's session with Lenora. What had they stated? . . . "Know that there is a Spark of the Divine with you, whether you are aware of it or not." I smiled to myself. So the secret hiding place of my own personal Father-God was finally discovered! . . . Right smack in the last place I would have ever suspected, in the very center of my mind! Subtle! I began to wonder how I might contact this marvelous, creative Source; how I might communicate with Him. Quiet and meditation were obvious prerequisites.

My thoughts wandered along, recalling the names of the guides for the Broome family. I must write them a letter soon. My heart warmed when I remembered "Belinda and Johnny," the little playmates of Lisa . . . Wouldn't Rick and Billie flip over this information? And 'Zuriel.' How the races of man could benefit from that one's speciality!

Then the next thought really jolted me! I almost dropped my cigarette. The true significance of that final cryptic statement now dawned on me . . . Somehow, Herod and Harold had foreseen my future! The words echoed again in my mind: "Sitting in the bathtub might help." I started to chuckle, then exploded with a roar of laughter that brought a nurse on the run. Wiping the tears out of my eyes, I barely managed to assure her that it was simply a little joke, nothing to get alarmed about. When she left, I wondered what the doctor would find written on my chart tomorrow.

Chapter IV

Tomorrow's Knowledge with Today's Wisdom

As I drove to Lenora's home for the next session (in August, 1971), I reflected upon something a friend had said to me. We had been on a trip to the high Sierra Nevadas, attempting (unsuccessfully) to locate the wreckage of a private airplane. We were returning, exhausted from high altitude hiking and climbing when I asked him several questions. His knowledge was extensive, and I found the conversation quite illuminating. Then, considering our recent failure to find the downed plane, I asked him if he might not be somewhat fed up with life on this planet, mindful as we were about the widespread ignorance, suffering, and limitations that surround us.

"Are you kidding?" my friend had protested, surprised. "Why, this has to be the most *fantastic 'school'* ever created!"

I recalled having sat silently for a long, long while, slowly digesting this stunning new concept. Imagine having a whole planet for a "school" to study in, to mature in, and to progress in! If true, it would explain much.

As I described the Sierra trip to Lenora, I found myself asking almost impatiently, "Is this planet really a 'school,' and are we here as students, with you serving as faculty?"

You have recognized the fact that many are there to help you at all times, those who are well aware of the pitfalls that you fall into, well aware of those which others have fallen into from time to time through the many centuries past. Do not be so hard on yourself. Be more gentle. Know that many beautiful things are coming to you, and through you. Continue as you go, and know that there is one at your side at all times to help and to guide you. It need not necessarily be those that you recognize, but this is not important. Continue.

Now a glimpse of the truth could be seen. "That rather confirms it," I said. "This planetary 'school' does have guides and teachers who invisibly help the human students. We can't see them because their vibrational frequency is too fast for our eyesight. Now I can see the technical meaning of 'spirit.' It means "ultrahigh frequency," and I'm wondering now if Harold and Herod can move faster than the speed of light."

It is <u>necessary</u>.

It seemed to me that this answer provided the key necessary to understand why a separation exists between "students" and "faculty" on this planet. The "ceiling" over the heads of human students—who dwell in physical-matter bodies—is the limiting speed of light, as taught in physics. And the above answer suggests that this same speed is the faculty's "floor," since they stated that it is *necessary* that they vibrate faster than the speed of light.

To confirm my theory, I asked, "Is the basic reason why we cannot see you due to the fact that your vibrations are faster than the spectrum of light that our physical eyes can see?

Yes . . . even faster than your mental vibrations. (There was a thoughtful pause) . . . to us, even your instantaneous is slow.

We both just sat there, gazing at each other. The impact of such an incredible statement, made so calmly, was beyond description. We took a break.

Lenora had been recalling more of the answers by now, so we had much to talk about. When we discussed the indwelling God-Spark, she remarked that many teachings had been given to reveal to humanity its true potential. Once fused with pure Source energy, it was said that even mountains could be cast into the sea. But few had believed.

Thinking back on the Divine Love that had been so freely bestowed upon those who had become One with the God-Spark, my heart began to ache. It was the paradox of being so close to my Creator, my Divine Architect, and yet not being able to bridge the chasm between mortal mind and the Pure Consciousness of my God-Spark, that caused my inner agony.

Turning wistfully to Lenora, I asked, "I don't suppose you could somehow get me a message—through Herod and Harold—from Him, from my Father-God?"

Lenora started, her eyes reflecting awareness of the magnitude of such a request. Glancing at the intense longing in my eyes, she suddenly relented and said she would try. She closed her eyes and waited.

There was a prolonged silence, to me like a breathless wait for eternity. When Lenora finally opened her eyes, they were overflowing with emotional tears and, very faintly, in the silence of a far, far dimension, I barely caught the precious few words:

●●●●●●

. . . . *He . . . sends . . . you . . . peace . . . and . . . love.*

●●●●●●

During August, 1971, I spent considerable time re-thinking what we had learned. Much had been absorbed, yet my impression was one of just beginning to understand the processes underlying humanity's progress in this remarkable planetary 'school.' Replaying the Lenora tapes over and over, I studied the subtle differences as well as the comparative phrasings and tones between the statements coming "through" Lenora versus her

own style of speech. There were several obvious points that
stood out. Whenever technical or scientific questions came up,
Lenora seemed "out of it," but invariably, the answers coming
"through" her seemed quite pertinent and concisely phrased.
Another point: Lenora seemed sometimes prone to doubts,
especially when faced with the implicit 'authority' in the tone
and content of their answers. Many times she had protested,
"Well, I wouldn't dare make such a statement, but that's what
they're giving!" In contrast, those who communicated through
her had no such qualms: their statements were highly intelligent, clear (to them), and fluent in a strangely "classic" style.
Sometimes, I felt much like a youngster who had wandered into
Einstein's private den, asking immature questions and trying to
comprehend gentle answers that often sailed over my head. How
could the youngster really appreciate the depth of such answers?
It became obvious that some of the viewpoints expressed
through Lenora were above the human perspective, such as
their calm indifference toward good and evil. When questioned,
they had simply answered:

━━━━━

*What child among you ever reached adulthood without
making mistakes? This is the only way in which true
growth can take place.*

━━━━━

Compared with the human tendency to call another 'stupid,'
they had used the delicate phrase: ". . . using less than one's
greatest wisdom," a far more gracious way to express it. Another
unique facet that reveals itself in their answers is the "essence of
practicality." For example, it had been learned that violence is
never condoned in their realm, yet when I broached the subject
of the human necessity to defend one's family, the answerer
wisely stated:

━━━━━

*As long as there are those who allow their sheep to stray,
others must build fences.*

━━━━━

Gradually, I came to understand that, somehow, Herod and
Harold could "see" into the essence of things. Their perspective

invariably extracted the "meat" from any subject. Still, we had also sensed their love of beauty and truth, their wisdom and patience, their acceptance and tolerance of all. There were times when I'd felt like sitting down with Lenora just to ask questions for days on end, but at the same time, I also realized that man must solve his problems at a pace that parallels his ability to comprehend. This vital factor was evidently well known by Herod and Harold. When Lenora and I discovered that both guides could literally "see" future probable events in a concrete manner, we asked them to describe some future event that could be checked. Probably smiling, they had wisely replied:

— — — — —

Then you would have tomorrow's knowledge with today's wisdom.
— — — — —

It was in the autumn of 1971 that I first slid into "Grogan's Gulch," my term for a state of depression. There were many factors which caused this plunge, not the least of which was a deep-seated sense of guilt over certain of my life experiences. It was all very well to intellectualize away such torments, but hidden in my subconscious was a child that could in no way rationalize these events and find release. In a word, I felt lousy.

One night, well after midnight, I lay back on the couch and closed my weary eyes. I'd been reading too much lately. Almost instantly, I began to dream very vividly. (This may have been an OOBE.)

The kitchen dishwasher rattled and buzzed loudly; the lower kickplate was loose again. Feeling an impulse to "fix it now," I got up from the couch and went into the garage to get some tools. As I entered the garage, I distinctly heard the sound of rushing water behind me. Thinking that one of the kids might have forgotten to turn off a faucet, I turned towards the corner that contained the washtub. Instead of the tub, my eyes focused on a very large, white toilet bowl! The water was churning and flushing as if the valve had stuck open! Numbly I turned around, glanced at Betsy (parked in her usual spot), at the workbench with all my tools scattered about, and knew that I was in my own garage, not someone else's. Then my sweeping eyes noticed that the garage floor was *green*, instead of the usual gray! Standing there, amazed beyond words, I felt a weakness in my legs. Then, slowly (like a slow-motion movie scene, only real), a powerful "force" turned me upside down in a smooth spiral and tossed me headfirst into the concrete floor! As I swirled into, and then right back out of the concrete, much like a child in a pool of water, I felt a warm tingle, an electric sensation throughout my body. Had I not been so stunned by the suddenness of it, I might have enjoyed this smooth romp though solid concrete. Then, just as suddenly, I found myself back on the couch, but "suspended" within my physical body! A gradual fusion then took place, lasting many seconds. I was able to feel the process as it developed and was deeply impressed by the exacting 'control' over this remarkable inversion into the flesh body. I then drifted into a deep, profound sleep.

The next morning I phoned Lenora to ask what might have caused the odd dream of the previous night, and why . . .

This was to show you the validity of that which you are studying: mind exists without the physical body; matter can be safely penetrated; green is the foundation or floor of understanding; and that which you believe are 'sins' can be washed clean in a twinkling. Do not be disturbed by these demonstrations. Continue with your seeking.

Now I began to understand. That whole series of events had not happened to shake me up, but merely to teach me something, something very valuable. Still, I wondered, who had manipulated such unusual power? When asked, the guides rather calmly and briefly reported:

This was your Divine Thought Adjuster, to help you understand.

At our next session, October 16th, 1971, one of Lenora's answers stated that man's mind is capable of controlling matter. Not yet having heard of Uri Geller, (who can mentally manipulate physical objects), I said that I rather doubted this answer.

Lenora asked why, so I described two attempts on my part that had proved to be total failures. Very early one morning, stumbling around in the dark, I had accidentally pulled on a pair of green socks instead of my usual black. These clashed with my suit so badly that, later on when I'd checked into a motel in another city, I attempted to transmute their color from green to black with the aid of an ancient formula extracted from some long forgotten book on alchemy. Then I went to bed, quite certain that when morning arrived, those socks were going to be black! I was thoroughly crushed when the alarm went off and I discovered that my socks were still as green as grass! Another time, I tried to infuse *prana*, or vital force, into a dying plant, one that I'd hoped to transplant from pot to the garden. The plant didn't respond in the slightest; it just wilted and died.

Lenora laughed at the green sock fiasco, then sobered herself and said she'd try to get an explanation as to why these experiments had failed. The interesting answer came:

━━━━━━

Were you doing this with the pure motive of proving that the energy is so, or were you doing this to see if you had the ability to do it yourself? It is important to stop and realize where this power comes from, and for what purpose you are putting it to use. Know that as you do these things with a real need at hand, with a real desire to help or benefit—and not to see the manifestation—then these shall come about . . . (pause) . . . it is not necessary that socks change color. Know that the plant may have lived its life and it was time for it to pass on. This is to help you recognize and realize the limitations that are within you, and yet as you turn more lovingly towards these things, they will manifest for you.

━━━━━━

Both Lenora and I well knew where the power comes from. Its "Source" is the Divine God-Spark within. As my thoughts turned in this direction, I felt another stab of remorse over my past mistakes, some of which had been beauts. (I'd done my best to make restitution, knowing that the physical act of making amends can be psychologically healing, but it turned out to be a

long process that ended only when I was introduced to meditation.) I asked if guilt or shame could prevent the mind from attuning to its Source?

――――――

*Only insofar as they are allowed to. They need not, for
there is nothing to be truly ashamed of, if man will recall
that all the things which he experiences are for his own
growth. Nothing is wrong, except those things which have
been allowed to be wasted, or to be reaccomplished, time
after time. If nothing is gained through an experience,
then it is a lost or wasted experience. However, if one
gains, no matter how shameful or wrong the situation
may appear, it is not something that he need hold to himself.*

――――――

Lenora added that they were showing her two symbol-
pictures. The first was: "Water Flowing Under the Bridge,"
washing white in the downstream rapids. The second: "The Spiral Staircase," that each person climbs step by step throughout
life. She said, "It's all right to look back down the staircase, to
evaluate the progress, but not to go back down there and re-live
past miseries." She added, "No high school student would think
of returning to grade school again." I agreed, feeling better.
"Experiential wisdom is just another term for, 'I've already been
down that old route.'"

I asked another question from my notes. "We humans sense
that our "I" dwells in the head, yet many books describe a 'soul
cord' that connects to the heart. What can be given as to this
apparent 'gap'?"

――――――

*The mortal "I," as you speak of it, is located in the con-
sciousness, which is in the head or the mind. This is the "I"
that you recognize. This is attached by an unseen cord to
the heart, for the heart is the seat of the emotion. The emotion is the true being of the soul, the true being of the person. This is why it is so extremely necessary to harness the
emotions, to be able to use them in a powerful way, rather*

than in a destructive way. The heart and "I" are one and the same, although in the human body they appear to reside in different spots. Know that the true "I" is the emotion in the heart.

● ● ● ● ● ●

We then brought up a possible problem area. How could humanity continue its normal way of life if there might be the possibility of being observed, and even recorded, from another dimension? Guessing that in an open, more universal dimension, privacy might be totally unknown, I asked: "What does the term 'privacy' mean to you?"

● ● ● ● ● ●

This would be those areas of life that are for that person, and for that person alone, to be right. It is not necessary that certain areas of your life be shared with any other one person, or any other group of people. There are those areas in all *souls, whether they be on the earthplane or in the "between" stages, or in the higher states. Know that* all things are *not* in common, *that there are areas and times and places for things to be* private.

● ● ● ● ●

I felt warmly reassured. They clearly recognized the right of privacy. However, no mention had been made of "recording" . . .

● ● ● ● ● ●

Know that these acts are a part of your own being. They are recorded within the realm of your own mind, for your own review at future times. These are some of the things which are not shared in general with others. This is not something that goes down as a cold hard "fact" into a "record." It is not a noting of minute detail, but the general things which go into a record are your own reactions to situations, your own feelings, your own thoughts about these things. Even these may go on about your own life, and then it is there for you to review at a later time. Do not feel that you are being intruded upon . . . such is not the case.

● ● ● ● ● ●

With great relief I remarked that it should have been obvious, from their gracious tact, that if humans had no wish to invade the privacy of others, how much more those who had advanced farther. Then I grinned, "Still, it's too bad that Herod and Harold don't pull up on the reins when I start to make some big boo-boo."

Why?. . . you would then not be able to define for yourself those things which you are doing. It is better that you learn through your own . . . . . boo-boo's . . . because then you are able to better adjust to your own thinking. If you were to be told, or to be stopped from doing certain things, then this would not help you to gain, nor would your inner strength come forth.

Lenora added, "This would be an excellent answer to those people who are forever asking, "Why does God allow pain, hurt, and suffering to afflict His children, if He truly loves them?" And also, there are some parents who might profit from such an answer, those who are afraid to allow their children to freely experience what life has to offer." I pointed out that to interfere with man's free will, his free experimental learning process, would negate the very purpose for which this planetary "school" was created. I continued with my questions, some of which probed the area of "power."

Is the principle that science terms 'laser,' or the stimulated amplification of light energy, the principle by which you use energies?"

We draw from even higher sources, and convert to that which is lower than ourselves . . . thus the condensing down . . .

It is only necessary to visualize the tremendous pressure available from a small spigot mounted near the bottom of a very large water tank, to see the area I was interested in probing. I had long been aware that "the higher you go, the greater the forces," such as the case of a steel crowbar which can be cut in two by a mere gas, (the acetylene cutting torch.) But higher still, a mere "light"—the industrial laser—can slice through steel like butter. Also, the laser can be adapted to extremely fine work, such as the welding of tiny eye tissues.

One evening at home, a golden-haired little boy appeared at the front door, shyly offering to sell baseball booster tickets. Heart melting, I went off to find my wallet. During the search, a scream of terror sent me racing back. I found that one of the dogs had slipped down the hall to see who had rung the doorbell. The boy was panic stricken, and nothing I could do or say seemed to calm him down. When the shaking lad finally departed, I (forgetting about negative karma) growled at the rest of the family about "untrained dogs" that went about frightening innocent little kids. When I eventually began to remember the possible negative reactions that might result from my negative growling, I exclaimed, "Oops!" and laid our biggest fire extinguisher on the kitchen counter in plain sight. I then warned everybody to watch out for earthquakes, fires, floods, the roof caving in, or any other possible catastrophes. The rest of that doubting bunch exploded with laughter. But three days later, the boomerang returned.

Chapter V

Adjusting to the Occasion

The switch clicked and lights blazed on in the barn. All morning I had been working at Baylands Stables where my daughters and their numerous friends trained their horses. I enjoyed lending my small knowledge of wiring and electrical circuits to old barns that needed attention, many of which had frayed wiring and broken switch-boxes.

Jack Brown, the co-owner, came by and asked me to take a look at Connie's Honda motorcycle. It badly needed tuning. I promptly got out my portable engine-analyzer and went to work. While I was putting the finishing touches on it, Connie approached and listened to the purring engine. She asked me to take it out on the road for a test drive.

When I returned, completely satisfied, I downshifted and slowly eased into the gravelly driveway beside the ranchhouse. Not being too experienced on smaller Hondas, I innocently tried to stop with the front handbrake and the bike suddenly slid out from under me with a crash! I fell on my left knee, tearing my workpants in the grinding gravel. As I fell, I shut off the Honda. Staggering up and lifting the unhurt bike, I felt a painful ache spread over the knee area, and blood oozed through the rip in my pants. The negative karma involving the dog now had its effect, I reflected. I limped into the house and asked Jack for a bandage and antiseptic, then went into the bathroom and removed my torn trousers. Turning on the hot water, I inspected the wound—five square inches of dirty, bloody hamburger—and frowned at the thought of the pain that would result from contact with hot soapy water. Then, like a flash-back, I recalled the hospital and the pain-control experiment. "What am I thinking?" I chided myself. "I don't have to suffer any pain! I'll just pull back on those "throttles" and block it!" Closing my eyes, I formed the mental image, eased back on the "throttles," listened to the "engines" die down slowly, then scrubbed away with the hot soapy washrag. Nothing!!! There was not the slightest trace of pain or feeling in the whole knee area! For twenty minutes I scrubbed out the dirt and grime, all the while elated that the pain control had worked so efficiently and smoothly.

Jack eventually returned and reported that he'd been unable to find a bottle of merthiolate. He'd picked up a bottle of iodine—used on the horses—but he didn't think I would use it. I grabbed the bottle and opened it as Jack warned seriously, "Man, that's gonna sting!" I grinned and said, "No . . . It *won't*! You remember awhile back I told you and Erma about my pain-control experiment? . . . Well, keep an eye on this!"

Dipping the swab into the yellow iodine bottle, I gave one more tug on my "throttles" (for good measure) and quickly splashed iodine over the red wound. The flesh quivered, but there was no pain, no sensation, nothing. Looking up, I had to laugh at the look on Jack's face. "Amazement" would seem inadequate to describe his transfixed wide-eyed stare.

The next morning, I consulted a doctor and received a tetanus shot. The wound healed rapidly but the scars remained for months.

The following weekend, Baylands Stables hosted a "Horse Show." Youngsters and their shining, prancing horses were milling around the stable complex; a rippling tremor of excitement spread contagiously. Shortly after the noon lunch break, Jack announced over the loudspeaker system, "LADIES AND GENTLEMEN . . . using the terms very loosely . . . AND

ALL YOU YOUNG WRANGLERS! . . . The next event, in the back arena, will be . . . JUMPING!" Amidst shouts of enthusiasm, I quickly turned over the snackbar to a young lad that worked at the stables, then joined Max Rhinehart as he headed out back to watch the spectacular event.

Max was co-owner of the stables, but his principal occupation was as a police officer. He was truly an intelligent, good looking, big-hearted guardian of the public welfare. Max had become highly interested in ESP and parapsychology, and many times had contributed cogent comments to the evening discussions at the ranchhouse. We have several times discussed "White Light" and its reportedly beneficial use in emergencies. Max confided that on one recent black night, when his unit had been dispatched to a riot area near Stanford University, he'd been faced with a group of furious, rock throwing agitators. Noting the possibility of serious personal injury, and yet not wishing to cause harm to the youthful rioters, Max had attempted to visualize a blazing ball of pure "White Light" around his position. Strangely, within seconds, the group in front of Max began to toss down their rocks and sticks and began to talk out their numerous grievances! Max had been startled by the sudden change. Looking up and down the street, he had readily seen that the riot was still in full bloom; but near his position, the atmosphere had become calm and rational. Max, after that episode, was a "believer."

As we walked, chatting about the size of the turnout, we suddenly stopped. Yells of anguish were echoing out of the rear barn, a huge old half-open structure. We immediately broke into a run, expecting to find an injured child or horse. Such was not the case. When we rushed into the barn, there stood nearly two dozen mothers with their small children, all quite distraught as they stared up at the high rafters. Glancing upward, we saw the cause of the commotion—a pathetic little pigeon had somehow gotten entangled with a yellow cord and was fluttering upside-down helplessly trying to escape.

"Get a ladder, Max!" one of the mothers called. Max looked up and gauged the fifty feet spanning the vertical distance to the pigeon. He called back, "There isn't any ladder around here that will reach that high." The crowd grew more agonized as the pigeon weakened with each flutter . . .

I desperately tried to think. I called Max over where we could speak privately, then suggested, "Why don't we try the "White Light," Max? . . . Instead of a *ball* of light, why don't we project a *beam* of light, like a white laser beam? If you can send it from one angle, I'll try to send from another angle, and maybe we can cut that cord and free the pigeon!" Max glanced around, noted the near panic and hysteria, then shook his head. "I don't think it will work here. That's pretty far out!" But, feeling a strong inner hunch, I insisted that it was at least worth a try. "Come on, Max! You've seen it work before! Where's your faith?"

Shaking his head, Max agreed to try. He walked back near the crowd—I stayed where I was. We both stared fixedly at the cord. I soon became aware that too much "negativity" was being generated by the crowd, so, to counteract this radiation, I called openly to Max, "Hey Max! It looks like that cord is starting to fray on the edge of the rafter! . . . I think it's going to break any second now!" (I knew the cord was nowhere near a rafter's edge, but the suggestion soon quieted the crowd. They all began to look up more expectantly.)

Several tense minutes crawled by. Both of us stood like statues, staring up at the cord. Finally, just as I was about to call it quits, everyone in that barn heard a distinct, sharp "snap!" and the little pigeon flew swiftly out through the open doors into sweet sunlight! A sustained "Ah-h!" went up from the now smiling, happy crowd, and several clapped their hands in delight. But the incredulous look on Max's face made me laugh out loud. His eyes were shining like saucers and his face was pink with excitement as he faintly stammered, "Dad, I-don't-*believe*-that!!!"

I was not naive enough to believe that either of us had done anything. We had mentally supplied a distinct 'signal' for higher help and, sure enough, 'they' had come through! The mental image of crossed white rays had signalled our guides for help, and the real (unseen) laser-like beams projected from a higher level had cut that cord with a resounding 'snap!'

Later that afternoon when Max described what he called "The Pigeon Miracle" to Jack and Erma, they both seemed surprised.

Erma mentioned that she had worked with those same cords and had never been able to break one. They were made of super-tough yellow nylon. She had seen the kids tie rocks onto the cords and throw them up into the rafters for fun.

On November 16th, with Lenora, I asked, "When one thinks White Light at something, to "purify" it (such as a sneeze or cough), how does one know that it is done properly? Could it inadvertently cause some unseen side-effects of a harmful nature?"

━ ━ ━ ━ ━

Purity is purity. *If one is cleansed or purified, it does not become contaminated or cause something to become impure—or to have side-effects—nor to have wrong attitudes clamped on.*

━ ━ ━ ━ ━

Lenora added that it felt like nothing was eradicated. Rather, it felt like "transmuted," or "raised" in vibrational rate. I said, "Oh, so that's what is meant by 'raising the vibes' of something! I wondered."

Probing the area of their arts, we asked questions related to music. Seemingly interested, the guides answered the question as to whether they ever joined together for group music with the following puzzler:

━ ━ ━ ━ ━

This is not necessary, though it can happen . . . the music is the mood.

━ ━ ━ ━ ━

I was amazed when Lenora described "chords" of music rippling forth from each individual seraph. To me, this was an entirely diffierent dimension. Imagine being able to outpour high-fidelity music whenever one wished! A blue mood might evoke a sad rendition of "Danny Boy"; a happy mood might produce a lilting, colorful Strauss waltz! My imagination soared with possibilities: the Music of the Spheres, then the thundering cadences of *Thus Spake Zarathustra* echoed through the inner halls of my mind.

I asked if anything describable could be given as to their recreational likes or dislikes. The answer came through with considerable brightness:

⬥➖⬥➖⬥➖⬥

Recreation to us is a being alert, a being "alive" . . . all things to us are as a recreation, for there is not a great deal of labor, in terms of what the earth would call labor. We do not do things that are physical in nature, thus all things become as mental gymnastics; and thus they are as a recreation to us. However, there are times of . . . lack of recreation, which would be our times of learning, of looking to the beyond, or absorbing those things which are as yet a struggle for us. This is as a work, and yet not again as a labor.

⬥➖⬥➖⬥➖⬥

Lenora stated that they were showing her the image of a baseball diamond, with the accompanying statement: "We do not play baseball." I puzzled over this, so she remarked that everything in their realm felt harmonious and peaceful; that there seemed no need for competition; that their creative nature expressed itself along higher lines of endeavor. I reflected, "Nice that they look at their work in connection with us as a recreation . . ." She replied that it seemed to be no burden to them at all.

I wondered what they looked like. I had scanned a few colorful plates, artists' renditions, in certain books on mythology, but there seemed to be many differing types. I asked, "If Herod were to look at Harold, would he see any 'light-bursts' in him?"

Lenora hesitated, then said, "I caught the phrase . . . "A twinkle in his eyes" . . . but just a minute now . . ."

⬥➖⬥➖⬥➖⬥

He appears as a series of light-rays to me. However, know that there is a more solid form underneath. The things that I am aware of are his actions and motives through the colors that I perceive.

⬥➖⬥➖⬥➖⬥

"Do we presume correctly then, that if Harold were to look at Herod, he would also see colors and rays?"

●━●━●━●━●

Yes . . . but his colors are more sharply defined than
mine. He is one who is more defined in his thinking . . .
not narrow, but clearcut.

●━●━●━●━●

Lenora and I chuckled and she murmured, "The Rainbow
Twins!" I then asked, "Why is it that the two of you function better together?"

●━●━●━●━●

It helps to keep any narrowness or ego out, for only as
these thoughts interact, backward and forward, are we
able to define the things which are more universal in be-
ing, without reflecting that which we would like to use on
our own. There is still many times the desire to project
through someone.

●━●━●━●━●

Lenora asked, "What did they mean by 'project through
someone'?" I smiled, "I think I'm beginning to catch on. The
other night I was just sitting quietly beside the fireplace, working on my notes, when out of thin air an 'inspiration' came into
my mind. I quickly jotted down the words and discovered a po-
etic quality to the phrases. I'll bet anything they projected that
poem to me! It's a strange little gem, but would you like me to
read it to you?" Eagerly nodding her head, Lenora said she loved
poetry.

THE BEETLE AND THE LADY BUG

Quicksand underfoot, a rock upon his back,
*   Lay a gloomy, grubby beetle, his thoughts an ebbing black.*
The more he clutched a foothold, the more he'd sink a bit;
*   The rock still pressed upon his back, nothing changed a*
*   whit.*
"There really should be answers to problems such as these,"
*   Mused the sinking little beetle, "Can someone tell me,*
*   please?"*
From up above, a cheerful Voice, of strength, of wit and love,
*   Said, "Take my hand, apply yourself, and let's together*
*   shove."*
Amazingly, the rock rolled off, the crushing burden gone;

The beetle straightened up to face the hope-filled rays of dawn.
Wading through the quicksand, toward the faroff banks,
He sought the Good Samaritan, to bless and give his thanks.
The unseen Voice, so clear and true, was as a beacon, shining bright;
Answers came, though rather deep, to guide him into pathways right.
When finally, the shoreline reached, the beetle looked around to find
The Voice, a gorgeous Lady Bug, with eyes of love and smile so kind.

Lenora exploded with laughter and, curious, I asked Herod and Harold how they perceived human laughter. They answered,

A warm pink shower upwards, the sound as a tinkle of broken glass . . .

During our conversation, Lenora mentioned that she sensed feelings of "enjoyment" on their part, that they had seemed appreciative of my rendition of their poem. Curious, I asked how they perceived the poetry. Their instant reply came as follows:

The ideas are with us, the words are heard, and yet we hear more than is put into words, for we see the full impact of those expressions which are used. This is a spot of beauty . . . becomes to us as a painting. Yes, we enjoy it thoroughly.

The movie *Born Free* had recently been run on television —the tale of Elsa the lion. Its message was that Elsa had to be returned to the wild country because she could not accept "civilized" ways. I asked if perhaps man also must regain the freedoms of the wilderness, rather than suffer restraints? And were the guides somewhat like benevolent Game Wardens?

This is to help you realize that all people have a place, all beings have a place. It is necessary that they be allowed to do that which comes to them on a natural plane. However, they do need to learn the discipline that goes with certain steps of progress. Yes, you might make this as a comparison . . . however, know that through all this, you are evolving and are growing towards the very capable game wardens yourselves.

We both thought this answer unusual. It hinted at the saying: "In my Father's house are many mansions," and also to the destiny of man. Thinking of the many, many different planes within unknown numbers of dimensions, I asked if all planets had this same multi-structured mode of life, or multiple planes of living realms?

Yes.

Then, thinking of the incredible complexities of the circuits in the brain, the intricate glandular and circulatory systems, all the chemical and hormonal interchanges, the coordinate integration of the organ complex, and the delicate subtleness of the sensory mechanisms, I asked if the human body was considered at all "exotic." An unusual answer came forth.

Exotic in that it has been created through a billion aeons of your time . . . not only on this planet, but on other planets . . . so that it has been perfected until it is at its present state. There are still imperfections within it, and yet it is something that has been developed for a definite purpose. It has extremely intricate design and working that has evolved through a trial and error process. All new innovations can be worked out over a period of time, but they do take evolving rather than transplanting or sudden changes such as an architect could instigate. Know that these are designed from a higher level, and the imperfections are witnessed, and are bred out.

I asked, "Much of our literature admonishes man to perfect himself. Why should we "storm the gates of heaven," or push evolution?"

●━●━●━●━●

You need not "storm the gates," but you must continue marching up the path toward the gate. You must find that there is a continuous searching, a continuous opening, a continuous expansion; for without this, man would be in the place where he appeared to be many centuries ago. There is this constant awareness that he is as a God within, and must begin to commune with this God and see things from his standpoint. Although this would seem impossible from the earth state, he must begin to try, and this is the reason he must flash his light in many corners.

●━●━●━●

"Is this 'searching within' accomplished somewhat more easily on other planets?"

●━●━●━●

Depending on the need of those who inhabit that particular planet. Those who are in need of the searching here, are those who have been placed here. None of this is by happenstance; none of this is by punishment.

●━●━●━●

Then I asked if Harold and Herod had ever served in a constellation other than ours:

●━●━●━●

Not as yet . . .

●━●━●━●

I reconsidered, then told Lenora, "I was going to ask them if, on other planets, the guides and mortals remain in telepathic contact."

●━●━●━●

Unless the lesser of the beings puts a halt to it, it is there. The mortal can tune it out, but the seraphim do not.

●━●━●━●

Pondering their "floor"—the speed of light—and realizing that some High Intelligence must have started to create from above that level, I asked, "I'm curious . . . Where did the ingenious concept of pulsing above-light speed energies into tiny spherical atoms—that link together to form molecules that form below-light speed 'matter'—originate? Did this come from the level of the Master Architects?"

Something strange happened then. Lenora receded, looking faraway, and waited for some time. The following came very, very slowly:

THE .. Master .. Architect . . . . . who .. helped .. to .. mold . . . create . . . originate . . . design . . . and .. perfect . . . . all. . that .. was . . . and is . . . and .. shall .. be . . . . the One . . . who . . . with His helpers . . . and instructors . . . . . begat . . . and began . . . all that is.

Amazed, Lenora protested, "How could this be? If God created everything in the beginning, how could He possibly have had Helpers and Instructors?" (I had to remain silent. Certain books might help answer her sincere questions, but there was no way that I could put into Time-Space word symbols the explanation of the Great Circle of Eternity. Eventually, she might read *The Urantia Book* or the *Upanishads* and absorb the knowledge that could lead to a glimpse of the reality of timeless, endless, never beginning, never ending, eternal existence.)

I turned a page and asked, "Would you kindly ask them why we must live with both good and evil in this realm; or positives and negatives, as some word it?" The answer returned clearly and forcefully:

It is necessary. *It is part of that which creates the "whole" . . . it is part of that which is necessary.* It must be, *for only through the* opposites *can anything come about. Without that which would hold something in place, there would be nothing to spin off into space for. It is* necessary."

Now we finally began to see. Without the potential for evil, there would be no way to "grow." Using the car battery as an example, it is well known that a car cannot be electrically started

unless *both* the positive and negative battery cables are connected, allowing the current to *flow*. Lenora thoughtfully remarked, "Yes. Without the mud, no lotus!"

Thinking about the freedoms in more advanced cultures, in
higher realms, I asked if Harold and Herod were 'fixed' in size.
Humorously, they replied:

◆━━◆━━◆━━◆

We have the ability to be that which is necessary. We are
able to be almost finite if necessary, and yet we can be far
more infinite when that, too, is necessary. We adjust to the
occasion . . .
◆━━◆━━◆━━◆

"Come on, Lenora," I protested, laughing. "How tall are
they? 'Finite' could pertain to a microscopic grain of sand, and
'infinite'? . . . " Lenora gazed into space for a few seconds,
then refocused on my grinning face. "Well, when they're con-
densed down nearest our level, they appear to be about six feet
tall. But they seem to 'expand' to about twice that size when
they . . . shift . . . or transcend into their higher levels, the
Thirteenth Plane." With a surge of admiration, I asked if we
would ever be privileged to meet them. The answer was not flip-
pant, but rather forcefully serious:

◆━━◆━━◆━━◆

Yes, but this will be in your dream-state. Do not discount
the dream-states, as these, many times, are more real than
your physical states.
◆━━◆━━◆━━◆

A few nights later, I got my first glimpse of the "colored rays."
It was not at all like what I'd imagined! Very early in the pre-
dawn darkness, I began to slowly drift up out of deep sleep.
Something aroused my wakeful awareness, yet my eyes and body
seemed still asleep. In this semi-dream state, I suddenly became
aware of a small circle of colorful "light" in the distance of space.
This "light" zoomed up to within three feet of my startled gaze
and began to "ripple" at me! This "light" consisted of a series of
seven concentric circles, or circular bands of neon-like colors—
transcendent red, golden yellow, azure blue, pink, orchid, and
silver. These light-circles were so brightly shining that I had to

look carefully to see the face within them. It was a beautiful face. The eyes were very large and loving, reminding me of a deer. Wide-spaced, they were set in a beautiful male head not unlike that of a gentle, wise, Grecian statue. The hair was dark, the forehead wide; arched eyebrows over large, subtly twinkling eyes that gazed back at me; a diminutive nose, a nice smile, exotically slanted cheeklines that flowed smoothly to an elfin, pointed chin; when viewed as a "whole" seemed utterly enchanting. A further surprise occurred when, between each circle of bright color, tiny lightning flashes began to pulse in sequence, rippling serially and radiating outward as if the intelligence within might be attempting to communicate with me! Whoever it was, he seemed quite cheerful . . . normal sized . . . and bright!

The very next week, I had another exceptional dream-event. I found myself standing on dry soil in desert country, facing an old weathered corral. Leaning casually against the corral railing was a gentleman—about six feet tall, garbed in a tailored, western-styled beige suit—who was speaking to me, imparting words of wisdom and good common sense. During this period, I curiously scanned his features. They were decidedly not human. Much like my first dream-episode, this visitor was extremely good-looking, (but minus all the colors), and had chiseled upswept lines to an exotic face that somehow reminded me of the famous actor, Charlton Heston. This visitor had a full head of dark, wavy hair, precision beauty of head formation, large gentle eyes, and a distant but friendly manner. He made no gestures, fully at ease. He spoke calmly but seriously about the reality of life in these other realms, that life is truly ongoing and eternal, and that no mortal had cause to worry about anything. I tried to pay attention, but standing in the presence of such a unique person . . . it wasn't easy.

Lenora was intrigued with my description. When asked to 'name' this gentleman-visitor, she for once forgot her hang-up and eagerly tried. She paused for several seconds, wide eyed, then abruptly refocused on my expectant face. "You're not going to believe this!" she declared. "It was *HEROD!*"

I was completely taken by surprise, having long forgotten the promise. The intervening weeks of family activities and job responsibilities had occupied my full attention. As the memory fragments began to collect and focus, my recollection of the former session sharpened. Still somewhat amazed, I murmured, "Well, for crying out loud . . . I should have guessed! I really should apologize, though, for not remembering all the good advice he gave me." An unexpected reply came through rather warmly:

That is all right . . . . you received the encouragement.

Lenora and I discussed this spontaneous display of kindness and understanding. We both felt a deepening appreciation for these remarkably gracious guides. It was guessed that the first meeting, (the circular rainbow colors that very likely displayed the guide's mental patterns), had been with Harold. And both guides may have transitioned through at least nine planes to meet with me on the fourth plane. I asked, "Why do you go out of your way to do these things?"

To enable you to complete your life-purpose, your chosen life-path.

"And can you reveal what this might be?"

To pull all the bits and pieces together and explode a myth.

Chapter VI

Zero Density = Instantaneous

In late December, 1971, a letter arrived from Colorado Springs, asking me to come visit them. It was from Rick and Billie Broome, the artist and his lovely wife. Rick's incredible space painting had so stunned our family, during its unveiling at Christmas, that for several minutes, no one could speak.

I immediately packed a suitcase that included the Lenora tapes, drove to the airport and hopped on a flight to Denver. On arrival, I phoned Rick from the air terminal and was somewhat puzzled when Rick said to hang on, that he'd be right up to get me within thirty minutes. Sure enough, about thirty minutes later, Rick arrived in a sleek, low-winged Cherokee. Climbing in, I greeted him warmly and, as we taxied out to the takeoff runway, asked when Rick had acquired his license. Rick chuckled, "I've had a license for several years, now. Just never mentioned it. Figured to surprise you one of these days. I often rent aircraft down in Colorado Springs, weather permitting." He turned, picked up his mike and requested takeoff clearance.

The sky was serenely clear and crisp, an open expanse of blue, during our flight south. I was impressed with Rick's smooth control of the Cherokee, his careful observance of the restricted areas near the Air Force Academy. His radio technique was clearly professional, yet his obvious love of flying was reflected in his relaxed attitude of enjoyment. Like all pilots, he knew the sky as a different world, a world of variables and peace.

Later, settling down in their snug, comfortable home, I proceeded to fill them in with details of the recent discoveries. They were listening to some of the tapes when Billie commented, "You can sure hear a difference in the style of speaking— Lenora's, and when the answers are coming through. It sounds almost as if she were 'reading' the answers." I agreed, saying that I'd become used to the changes when I realized that the answers had to be coming from a source other than Lenora.

The discussion turned to the subject of "rebirth." I likened the process to a millpond paddle-wheel whose paddles (i.e., "lives") each spent only a small portion of time beneath the water (i.e., in the flesh), and it had been stated that each individual had been placed on this planet for individual growth needs. The assumption followed that each individual came from some other planet or system to enroll in this highly intense "school of growth."

Little Lisa gently tugged on my arm, silently competing for attention. Sweeping her into my arms, I asked if Santa Claus had brought her some nice presents at Christmas time. With a wide-eyed glance, she pointed straight up and exclaimed, "Ho!-Ho! on the *roof*!!!" I glanced at Rick and Billie who lay back convulsed with laughter. The explanation came that sly old Rick had hauled some sleigh-bells up on the roof, Christmas eve, and had loudly called, "Ho! Ho! Ho!", jangling the bells with all his might.

Opening a book I had brought with me, *Psychic Discoveries Behind the Iron Curtain,* we studied both the text and photographs pertaining to a unique energy-substance which had been named "bioplasmic energy" by its most recent discoverer, Dr. Kirlian. His photographic, radio-field technique had uncovered a unique phenomenon: that even when a flower bud was sliced in half and one physical part was removed from the scene, the bioplasmic energies could still be photographed, as if the energy pattern had remained coherent!

I explained, "Plasma is a fourth state of matter: solid, liquid, gas, and plasma. Plasma differs from a gas in that it conducts electricity and is therefore affected by magnetism. Collected quanta of energy must have some magnetic field or *coherent* (organized pressure-pattern) *form* in which to function. An analogy might be the vapor in cloud patterns: non-coherent clouds are like high, stratified cirrus types; semi-coherent cloud patterns are like cumulus cells that build and rise in clusters; but coherent cloud forms are usually found only in tornado funnels and lenticulars, the "cap-clouds," and these exist only in well-defined pressure areas which mold the pattern-forms."

"Are you implying that some type of "duplicate magnetic form" must exist inside a physical object?" Billie asked. Pleased, I replied, "Precisely so, and here's another sample. When half of this leaf is physically removed, one would expect a subsequent photograph of its corona to show just the remaining half. But as you both see, this second photo shows a corona exactly like the first, the whole leaf. So despite the fact that half the leaf was removed, the whole outline in the second photo reveals that a complete and coherent energy pattern-form still exists within and behind the outer physical leaf. From this we can postulate the existence of bioplasmic "duplicate forms" within all known physical objects, which of course include our physical bodies."

Spontaneously, Rick exclaimed, "That may be the explanation to the question of why amputees can feel various sensations, even when a limb has long since been removed. They could be feeling aches and tingles in the bioplasmic limb!" "That's a really good point, Rick . . . Wish I'd thought of that. Also, this finding could supply the answer to the question of conscious life after death. It should be obvious that consciousness must have some "vehicle" in which to function as a separate individual, apart from the ocean of Infinite Consciousness. If this bioplasma is an energy-substance, and a "duplicate" of the physical body, there's your vehicle for ongoingness!" I leaned back and relaxed.

Billie wistfully remarked that this news didn't sound so nice for the elderly, those who were crippled. If this bioplasmic body was a "duplicate" of the physical body, wouldn't these people

"transfer over" and continue to live with their former miseries?
"I think not!" I replied. "We've already begun to unravel that
one. Harold and Herod have stated that mind can control matter. Now I'll concede that 'physical matter' is evidently too dense
to be readily controlled with the mind, although there are many
cases of couples gradually becoming 'look-alikes' over the decades. But it seems obvious that the less the energy density, the
easier the mind control; such as, clay is easier to carve than
rock."

Ignoring Billie's twinkly remark about the rocks in her husband's head, I turned to the tape recorder and put on the "Marvin tape," explaining that this youngster had "transferred over"
to the other side when he was five years old. He stated that he
was now eight, and had been openly eager to talk with a group of
researchers through a talented, motherly channel. Information,
data, and descriptions of his life and happy activities had been so
delightfully innocent that tape-copies had been sent to other interested parties.

Rick and Billie listened carefully to Marvin's chatter. He
answered the questions openly, even though he had some
difficulty trying to describe his activities in a way that would
make sense to the listeners. We could feel the gears turning in
Marvin's head, and we chuckled once when he flatly stated:
"Gee! . . . I   dunno! . . . I   could   ask   my   teacher,
Herothophy!" Most of the time, he seemed quite sure of his
statements. One question from the group had probed into his intended length of stay in his present environment. Marvin said
that he planned to, "Stay full time, not hurry back like those
(who were) on a lower level." Asked what level he was on, he replied, "Da fourth," and that the others who seemed in a hurry to
get back into physical life are on the "first level." (Evidently each
Plane contains many levels; some books suggest seven.) Asked
what "full time" meant, Marvin replied, "Forever, if I wan-
na . . . but sooner or later, you go back down." Asked about
his school, he happily reported that he lived in a dorm, that his
roommate was Eric ("But he's a *big* boy . . ."), and that his
happy, cuddly mother came to play and visit with him often.

Continuing, we listened as Marvin said no, his mother didn't visit his room (and he laughed impishly), "Cuz da alligator might get her!" Explanations followed that Eric had a pet baby alligator. Asked if the alligator ever bit Marvin, he exploded with laughter and replied, "Nah . . . Eric, he puts a rubberband around her jaws, and she won't bite you!"

Asked what he was learning in school, Marvin replied, *"Lot's* of things!" Could he give an example? He said, "W-e-ll, take Timmy. When Timmy transformed (moved up a grade?), he wanted *books* for his present . . . Timmy loves books! . . . So he got twenny-four books! He was so happy, he took 'em to *bed* with him!" Patiently, the group asked how these books applied to classroom activities, and Marvin explained, "W-e-ll, he had to *be* everybody in da books after he read 'em." Then he added very sorrowfully, "But when he got to da parrot, nobody would let him come on dere shoulder, so . . . he never got to be da parrot."

It was with some difficulty that the listeners unraveled what Marvin was describing. What eventually emerged was that these young students were being taught the fine art of "form changing." Timmy had read a book similar to *Robinson Crusoe*, then in class had to "be" (i.e., "change his form to that of . . ."), the Pirate, Crusoe, then the parrot. But Timmy's rendition of "da parrot" had been too sharp-clawed, and ". . . nobody would let him come on dere shoulder." Marvin described it as learning to "unfold."

Although there was more, I stopped the tape to try to make a point. It was becoming obvious that the rarer the realm's density, the less effort required to change forms with the mind. The physical realm is quite dense. But in Marvin's realm, where the energy-level is less dense, their minds might be quickly trained to "change" form, finding less resistance than in our physical realm. (This in no way lessens the apparent solidness of objects in other realms, however. It was later stated that a fourth-level piano can be played exactly like one in our realm, by those in fourth-level bodies.) The probable answer to Billie's wistful question was twofold:

First, that no person—no matter what the physical condition—need worry about transfer into higher levels with the same handicaps. ("Higher" means higher frequency spectrum only. It has no reference whatsoever to "up" or "height." This is more like changing television from VHF to UHF.) The combination of desire and imagination, "image-in-ation," are the tools with which less dense energy-forms may be re-formed, or "transformed" into whatever bodily form one might desire . . . (even da parrot!) A remarkably warm and interesting book by Don and Thea Plym, *2150—The Macro Love Story,* covers these and other aspects rather well.

Second, stresses are known to inhibit the clarity and efficiency of the mind. Transferring over may unstress the nervous system to some degree, much like the person who leaves an uptight job for a new, more promising job. The newly released energy from "taking a break" for a time might easily strengthen and clarify the mind. The combination of more easily controlled energy-substances in higher realms and a more powerful mind, might easily account for Marvin's unique classroom activities.

As a favor to Rick and Billie, I had brought along a message from their guides. Lenora had contacted them with no difficulty. The taped message was one of warm encouragement and cheerful hope for the future. They advised the Broomes not to worry over their plans for a new split-level home, that this would not prove to be a financial hardship or embarrassment for the family. (This came true, along with other items.)

That evening, Rick and I drove into town to take in a movie. Billie declined, preferring to remain home and watch television with Lisa. It was after midnight when we returned, said goodnight to each other and went to bed. Silently entering the guest bedroom, I was startled to see a "message" resting on the pillow. 'Wow!' I thought, "They really did it this time! . . . Actually materialized a piece of paper on my pillow!" With slightly shaky hands, I picked it up and carefully examined the message. It was penciled in a strange style, a few misspelled words, and sort of left-handed or slanted. I deciphered as much of it as I could, then climbed into bed and fell fast asleep.

The next morning at breakfast, the mystery was cleared up when Billie related the strange events of the previous evening.

Not long after Rick and I had gone out, she had commenced cleaning up Rick's art studio. She had been mentally pondering how best to communnicate with me during my visit. At the time, she had several items in hand—pencils and paper. As she went past the dining table, she unexpectedly 'sat down' and felt her arm go numb all over. Then she watched with amazement as her arm picked up the pencil and wrote a letter! When it was finished, her arm became 'all tingly' for nearly thirty minutes. Curious, she then read the following:

These are great mind opening times for you three. Communicate freely and openly about mortal problems, for only mortals can understand truly the drives of other men. Good can come from this beyond your comprehension. Try not to let our presence interrupt your free thoughts, as those thoughts are yours and only yours, as you know!!! Help each other. This is a basic need. Use this now. You have been brought together for purpose. Communicate, communicate, communicate.   Love and Peace

Billie added that after this unusual event, she'd watched her hand turn the page over, start to write something further, then pause and vigorously erase what had been written! I turned the page over and carefully examined the back side. Sure enough, the erasure marks could be discerned across the top of the page. We held it up to the light, tilting it so that the light might reveal the extremely faint letters and words. Finally I deciphered:

You three are children of light. I can say no more.

Billie further stated that she had been flabbergasted by this unusual method used by her guides to communicate with her. She and Rick had warmly accepted their comforting presences, including little Johnny and Belinda, but she'd never before displayed any talent for "automatic writing." Then, thinking that I might be interested, she had placed it on my pillow.

'Interested' isn't quite the word. I said firmly, "Remarkable!" Rick's expletive was a long drawn out, "FAN . . . TASTIC!!!"

Two weeks later, I was relating to Lenora some of the details of my recent visit with the Broomes. When I described how Billie had asked (mentally) for advice, and how her arm had been used to write the message, Lenora exclaimed, "That's exactly how I started! Then the impressions came into focus and I was helped to 'unblock' and let the words flow on through. Oh, I'm so happy for Billie!" (I didn't mention it then, but it had been during that particular trip that I'd first met Rick's mother and learned that Billie's true name is "Marsha.")

The January, 1972, session began with a question about rebirth. "Does each soul have a choice as to which planet he or she will next live on?"

Not always, for there are times when the needs have not yet been fulfilled, or the growth is not quite to the extent that it can progress to another planet, and yet there are times when it needs to be sent to one specific area for the growth that can come in that way. After one has reached a certain stage of growth, they can then pick and choose to some extent. It would also depend on the lessons to be learned. If there were a choice of lessons, they might choose the planet. This again is very individualized.

"Does each soul have a choice as to which sex it will become?"

Usually yes, for there is a set pattern that one can follow. However, if one chooses to take on male aggression with a female body, they will find that they have more than coped with the problem at hand. There are times when a soul will take an extremely difficult challenge, and thus it can run into many errors or problems. This is part of the learning process. There are mistakes made here, but they are not of an irreparable nature.

"Does each soul have a choice as to which specific karma (the results of past causes), and how much karma it will next take on?"

Yes. This is a matter of pure choice, and the soul again may not extend its greatest wisdom; for there are times when some overextend their capabilities, or try to erase too much karma in one life. This can be dangerous, but they are allowed to take on that which appears to be right. This is the case when some souls begin to diminish or blank out their thoughts, and thus become closed. They no longer expand or grow, even though life goes on . . .

━━━━━━

"Are there counselors available to help and advise?"

━━━━━━

Always . . . but there are those souls who will exhibit their own independence and feel they know themselves better than those who counsel. Those who counsel are not of a restrictive nature. They present a plan, but the soul may choose another.

━━━━━━

I sat still, absorbed in my thoughts, trying to visualize this new concept of freedom in higher realms. It was difficult for me to realize that I had freely chosen this life of struggles and hardships. And who knew what else I had planned for the future? I could ask my guides, but they would surely answer with that famous, "Then you would have tomorrow's knowledge with . . . ", and I'd probably go out and get drunk and head for Mexico and . . . "Lord," I quietly thought, in mock self-pity, "It sure would be nice to retire to some peaceful, quiet cave somewhere . . . "

Suddenly, they seemed to answer my thoughts with a curious, delicate:

━━━━━━

Would you become a monk?

━━━━━━

I was startled, not yet accustomed to the fact that my guides were telepathic, and that my thoughts (to them) were like a conversation. I almost started to frame a reply when the following was strongly advised:

━━━━━━

No! . . . Immerse yourself in life!

━━━━━━

During 1972, I discussed with Lenora the two new books by Jane Roberts, *The Seth Material* and *Seth Speaks*. This latter had been dictated through Jane to her husband, Robb, by a high teacher in another realm (Seth), and reveals a considerable amount of information about life in other realms and the transition through so-called death.

At my first reading of these brilliant works, I couldn't figure out just what Seth was, or what his position might be with relation to known levels of consciousness. Guessing that Seth might be the 'superconscious' self, but not really sure, I decided to do some research into some of the older books on my shelves. I selected Max Freedom Long's *The Secret Science Behind Miracles*, one of the old favorites. Max had written of the long years of effort it had taken him to break the secret code of the Polynesians. They had never developed a written language, but utilized a basic oral language for the people and a symbolic, hidden language for their priests, or kahunas, (which translates: Keeper of the Secrets). These priests had evidently found access to "powers" beyond man's present understanding. Max personally witnessed weather control, shark control, and among other fascinating events, rapid healing of both a physical and psychological nature. On this latter point, Max discovered that these priests were cognizant of the Three Selves: the Low Self (Unihipili), described under cryptoanalysis as a "clinging spirit" or one like a younger brother or sister who "sticks to . . . ;" the Middle Self (Uhane), the talkative one; and the High Self (Aumakua), the superconscious self. And here was where Max's breakdown and concise interpretation of the syllables and polysyllables within this term became fascinating. The word 'Akua,' in Hawaiian, means a 'god,' and the addition of 'Aum' signified something far more meaningful to the searcher. The 'Au' had one meaning, the 'um' another, 'mak' added more meanings, 'aku' still more, and so on, until the word ended and the description was completely revealed. The full meaning of the title, 'Aumakua,' was finally and surprisingly decoded as:

━━ ━━ ━━ ━━ ━━

The older, wiser, kind and loving, utterly trustworthy, Father-Mother God.

━━ ━━ ━━ ━━ ━━

Although these priests were aware of even higher 'gods,' (Ku, Kane, and Kanaloa), they made no effort to comprehend such transcendental heights. They simply focused their reverence and love on their Aumakua. These priests reasoned that any prayer-request beyond the capacity of their High Self god would be passed along to a higher god for appropriate action. This simple faith, inner guidance, and help from the High Self brought many of them very close to Unity, the goal and fulfillment of all religions, the very goal of time-space life itself.

I asked Lenora, "Is the soul-being, or what Seth calls the 'whole self,' a combined sex, or what might be termed 'unisex'?

━━━━━

Yes.

━━━━━

"Does the soul-being have a high degree of intelligence?"

━━━━━

Always.

━━━━━

"Seth would certainly seem to have a high degree of intelligence. Is he, perchance, a High Self . . . an Aumakua?"

━━━━━

One and the same.

━━━━━

So, it all connects up beautifully!, I thought happily. Seth must be known to Herod and Harold, else they would not have answered so firmly. But why had Seth not dictated anything about those like Harold and Herod? . . .

━━━━━

These teachings were slightly veiled, so as to reach a wider audience.

━━━━━

Seth had proven brilliant, witty, charming, and humorous. I wondered about one odd quip, though. Seth had called one of his personalities, Frank Withers, a "fathead." When I asked, Lenora laughed merrily and said she'd try to get an explanation.

━━━━━

This was an understanding between the two. This was not intended as a difficult thing, but (was) of a joking nature.

━━━━━

One of the book's major points is that mortals do not live lives in succession—in chronological order—but that all one's lives are being experienced simultaneously; that man is a multi-dimensional entity. Sensing that here was a real mystery to be solved, I asked about "Time."

"What is the mechanism that enables 'growth in time' within a Universe All, where "All IS" . . . ?"

●━━●━━●━━●

You are in a subject that is very intriguing. You have reached the point of desiring to know why, how, and when all things are . . . (pause) . . .

There is a "sense of time" within the mortal mind, for mind is also "thought," and thought is a "movement." Thought must have something to peg, or log by. Thought is a movement which "causes" time to "be."

Without thought, all things "are." Without processes, time "is." Time is only a measurement which man insists upon, that he might improve the rate of his own growth. This is something which was built into the universe for the mortal mind, for those who would need a "yardstick."

All and eternal are forever . . . this means that though there "appears" to be time, those who have reached the "ultimate" are in a state of "nonflux." They are not aware of time as passing, for to them, time has ceased, and yet still "is." This would be the nearest that we could come to explaining this in a logical form for you. Only as you progress in the particular earthly existence that you are now in, are you aware of time as hours and minutes, days and years. You will find that even when you are in the interim state between lives, you will not be as aware of time, or its "passage," as you are now. For even as one learns in that particular existence, they will find that there is an expansion of knowing without the sense of months and years.

●━━●━━●━━●

Now we began to see the "difference." Harold and Herod dwell in a very rarified energy-realm, a 'non-flux' dimension, whereas humanity dwells in a much, much denser energy-realm. We visualized birds flying swiftly through the medium of the air, whereas fish must swim more slowly through the medium of water. Then the "density of the medium" had to be the governing factor of speed; ergo, the denser the medium, the slower the speed. I asked, "Is it not true that consciousness functions more rapidly as its 'medium' becomes less dense?"

━━━━━

Consciousness "is." There is not a time, nor a place, nor a necessary element, as far as thinking . . . or construing something . . . (pause) . . . Time "is," in the conscious state.

━━━━━

"Well, is it not true that consciousness, functioning in my brain . . . "

━━━━━

Slows down . . .

━━━━━

"Right!" I continued. "It functions more slowly than it would on your level. This confirms what I was thinking, that 'thought-movement' is *relative* to the *density* of the *medium* in which it functions."

━━━━━

True, and yet it is difficult to explain that in "conscious-ness," there is not *a thinking "process" . . . . . the process "is."*

━━━━━

Lenora added that they were showing her something "immersed," but not "moving" (perhaps like a fish in a still lake, rather than a fish in a flowing river of 'time'). She also said they were showing her a tall lighthouse tower; that if one were down 'inside' that tower, one would have to look out through one window-slot at a time, and one after the other, to get a glimpse of the view; but if one were standing on the top of the tower, one could easily see all over.

I continued pondering, trying to figure out how they could "think" without "thought-movement" (?) . . . As if trying to help, they suddenly said:

━━━━━

Thought movement is something that proceeds within the conscious mind when it is in the "waking state." This is the logical stream of thinking that is necessary for mankind

▬ ▬ ▬ ▬ ▬
This is what children are trained to do. This is what adults rely upon.
▬ ▬ ▬ ▬ ▬

I interrupted with, "Well, when Harold and Herod telepathically communicate, aren't thoughts bounced back and forth between them?"

▬ ▬ ▬ ▬ ▬
There are many things which are understood because they "are." They do not have to be "bounced back and forth," as you put it, but there are occasional realms or areas where one is a little more versed or knowledgeable than the other, and in this case they send the thought in an understandable "picture-feeling" manner.
▬ ▬ ▬ ▬ ▬

Like a bulldog, I refused to give up before I thoroughly understood what they were driving at. I sensed that I was on the verge of a momentous discovery. It would not do to try their patience, but to pass up such a chance as this simply wasn't my nature. Once again, I continued pondering:

"Since thought movement must have some 'medium' in which to move, one could postulate that, 'As the medium becomes less dense (or more rarified), towards zero density, thought movement might become near instantaneous . . .'"

(Lenora instantly flashed:)

▬ ▬ ▬ ▬ ▬
True . . . and this is what we are trying to help you reach the point of knowing, that consciousness "is"; that this is a point where all things are. It is neither forward nor backward, nor in logical order. It just "is."
▬ ▬ ▬ ▬ ▬

The light finally dawned! I leaned back and wondered aloud, "Now why didn't I see that before? *Our* consciousness has to pulse from cell to cell along the neural pathways in the *physical brain* (its 'medium' for thought processes). But Herod's and Harold's consciousness *need not pulse at all!!* Their realm is so rarified that it could be considered *zero density*, and with nothing to *impede* thought movement, thoughts become *totally instantaneous*, or "no thought movement at all." This must be what they mean by the phrases: "Consciousness IS," and "All IS!"

After a short breather, we recalled the humor connected with my episode in the sitz bath, so I resumed by asking how they could 'see' the future, those events which had not yet happened in our realm:

We know all the things that "are," and are "coming" . . .

(Lenora said that the word "coming" was very tiny, and it was as if the "coming things" are NOW).

We see the way that man is becoming . . . we realize the outcome. We know those things which he is bringing upon himself in his own time, but to us it appears as "now."

There is the possibility of changing these things, if man feels suddenly inspired to become as a different one, or takes a sudden turn that seems to change his life. This, then, changes even the "now," so that those things which appear to us, change at that instant, so that we again see that which "will be" to man.

From this last statement, we were able to see that each of us does have 'free will,' that no one is locked onto a predestined treadmill. Higher sight might be regarded as a "total perception" of time-space events which appear to "time-space minds" as single, successive events. Higher sight is an overview of time-space, a totally inclusive perspective of time-space pageantry.

In order to understand how the seraphim can view such in-depth scenes, several working examples can easily be constructed:

A parallel line of fish are swimming upstream at the same speed the river flows downstream. To the fish, much "time and motion" progress is obviously taking place; but to an observer who stands 'high' on the riverbank, the fish are relatively motionless (i.e., with respect to forward or backward movement). One can realize how easy it is for the riverbank observer not only to see those logs (events) that have floated downstream "past" the line of fish, but also see the logs that approach the fish from upstream (the future). One should note that each fish does have the freewill to choose to suddenly turn and perhaps avoid an upcoming collision. Another example, perhaps more suited to westerners, is the guide who stands on top of a steep mountain peak, observing to his left the beginnings of a rockslide. Down below, to his right, along comes a cowhand who is riding around the base of the mountain into the path of the "future" rockslide. If the cowhand were warned to 'hold up,' he would have the freewill choice of either heeding the call or ignoring it, and in this latter case, would continue around the mountain. Needless to say, his last earthly thought could very well be, "Wonder how the heck that voice up there could see the future so easily?"

Still, something was missing. What kind of impersonal self control would it take to be able to see future catastrophes approaching, yet withhold any trace of warning? (Or is it that humanity's progress towards the development of telepathically 'hearing' such warnings has been repressed by those who fear new advances?) Either way, how could those with such a high perspective remain totally optimistic about man's accomplishments and the final goal, since wars and destructive struggles seem to continue throughout known history? Soon, late one evening, a possible answer came to me by way of 'inspiration.' I was quietly working on my notes when a NEW PERSPECTIVE came into mind:

There at the rear kitchen window stood gazing the wise, experienced mother. She casually observed her children playing in the mud, building their mud castles. Yes, they became grimy and dirty, sometimes fought and argued, sometimes smashed one another's mud castles. Sometimes they threw mud at each other like it was going out of style. But does she ever once consider her children "evil"? Not at all! The wise, patient mother knows that all children must "grow" to adulthood, and their childish play is a natural process of daily growth. She also knows that when she calls them in at the end of their play period, she can plop them into a tub of warm water, clean them spotless, put fresh clothing on them, and they will then be as fresh and shining as they ever were . . . AND ONE DAY WISER! It could only be through such play periods, both happy and sad, of error and success, that each child could learn to guide itself. The wise mother knows that knowledge can be shared, but not wisdom. Wisdom comes only through experience. The wise mother, having repeated the process many, many times before, does not rush out and interfere with her children every time a fight starts. This would only delay the "learning processes" and interrupt the lessons that each child must learn before entering adult life.

Like a returning echo from the past, I remembered the answer:

●━●━●━●━●━●

What child among you ever reached adulthood without making mistakes? This is the only way that true growth can take place.

●━●━●━●━●━●

The reflections continued, expanding towards deeper understanding of humanity. In many areas of life on this planet, there would seem to be too much 'push' towards perfection, far too much emphasis on 'being perfect NOW,' rather than growing slowly and surely towards that goal within the very Time-Space framework that has been created for humanity. And are we the 'kids' playing out in the 'backyard'? If the wise human mother loves her kids, despite all the mud and dirt, how much more the infinite Love of the Creator of all?

One might think, 'But kids get killed out in this backyard!' One should perhaps think again. Hurt, yes; killed, no. All teachings clearly imply that life is truly eternal and ongoing, forever.

If the wise human mother has the patience and courtesy to allow her kids to gradually mature to adulthood, and not to judge them as adults until they have grown up, then how likely to assume that the Creator will withhold His judgement until His children will have 'grown up' in future eternities? It goes without saying that premature judgement in a world of constant change is very like a dog chasing its own tail. And the Creator is wise, not foolish.

Much historical evidence indicates that the Creator of All is constantly aware of all His backyard 'play areas,' and particularly this tiny experimental planet, since down through the ages many older Brothers have been sent to try to 'cool it,' to help humanity 'see' more clearly the nature of Creation, to show humanity that unlimited potential lies within each one of us.

But time reaps its toll and man loses the knowledge of his Source. Then disbelief forms a barrier around the mind and eventually around the heart. Such a barrier prevents pure energies from infusing the human being with energy, and the mind gradually weakens. As it weakens, man becomes less able to meet the demands of his environment. Then man commences to suffer.

There is no known method of strengthening a mind from some 'outside' energy source. The source of Pure Energy is said to be hidden within man, and this fact is now being empirically rediscovered by medical research. Control groups of non-meditators and meditators have been carefully tested over a period of years and the evidence shows that meditators significantly outshine non-meditators in many fields of endeavor, including personal health and well-being, the arts, business, science, interpersonal relationships, education, and environmental happiness. Educators worldwide are becoming enthusiastic over the statistically meaningful increase of I.Q. that results from a simple technique of "turning within" twice a day. The easiest method known is Transcendental Meditation™.

Chapter VII

The Silver Shadow

The meeting with Lenora during March, 1972, proved quite fruitful. I had decided to find out all I could about the seraphim and those who live in adjacent planes. When I asked Lenora if she could find out where most people went when they 'transferred over,' she paused, then said she was getting a "Four" and a "fourth." This evidently meant the fourth plane of the Fourth Dimension, which is also called the Astral Plane. Then I asked:

"During the 'between life' stages, is there individual progression from plane to plane? Lenora promptly answered, "Yes."

"Those objects that we recognize as towns, parks, rivers and lakes, fish and birds . . . are all these things in the other planes? Are these *real* worlds that people dwell in?"

━━━━━

Yes . . . but not in the physical matter that you would see it, or feel it, and yet it appears to be just as solid to those who are existing in that particular plane; for their density is such that the density of the items around them appears to be of equal density. ━━━━━

I was happy with this answer. This was exactly the way I had figured it—it was all relative to the individual's "body." I recalled the "piano" example: that if a man's body were composed of "plane four" energy-substance, he could sit down and play a "plane four piano" just as easily as one in this physical-matter realm, (assuming he knew how to play a piano, of course). It also meant that to all those people who have transferred over, the objects in their environments are *real* and *solid.* Then I asked:

"Can people in those other realms use telepathy?"

● ■ ■ ■ ■ ●

Always. *It is assumed . . .*

● ■ ■ ■ ■ ●

We were surprised at the openness of this answer. That such a "gift" would be simply assumed by others had never occurred to us. I asked:

"After transferring over, can a person faint?"

● ■ ■ ■ ■ ●

There is no need, for those in the physical body faint from lack of being able to cope with the situation, or because there is a physical problem. This is not continued in the higher realm.

● ■ ■ ■ ■ ●

There had seemed some reflected amusement in Lenora's voice during the answer. She was gazing at me rather oddly when she said, "You can sure think of some odd questions! Who'd have ever thought of such a thing?" I shook my head, smiling, then asked a more serious question:

"What is the mission of the seraphim, for mortals?"

● ■ ■ ■ ■ ●

More of a "framework setter," as those who see a general plan and know when things become out of balance with that plan. There is a guarding against, or a pulling together of those necessary facets to be able to complete a life cycle or life plan, but there is not a force of energy nor an impelling need here.

● ■ ■ ■ ■ ●

Lenora described seeing "squares" that surrounded each person, that if certain things were needed, the seraphim could pull from some squares to help complete others, or to 'set the stage' properly. I suddenly realized just what the answer meant. Several weeks earlier I had returned home to find my wife upset. The high school had just informed her that one of our daughters had not been to school for two solid weeks, unable to face it any longer. We both felt helpless, having tried twice before to help this daughter over an unusual psychological problem. We had been unable to get school counseling. We'd even changed schools for her, but she withdrew after a short stay. After unsuccessfully attempting to communicate with my daughter, unable to bear her tears of frustration, I thought of Lenora. Surely this daughter had guides; perhaps Lenora might be able to get some helpful advice, or at least discover the cause of her problem. When I phoned, Lenora sympathetically said she'd be glad to help. She listened, then said they were saying that the daughter's problem was a subtle form of claustrophobia, that the child had been trying for years to cope with it. But eventually the four school walls just 'closed in' on her. She said they were advising the seeking of school counseling, to ask for a "home teacher," that in the familiar surroundings of her home, the child would feel secure and do much better. I said we would try, and thanked Lenora very gratefully. I relayed this advice to my wife, and despite some misgivings as to the outcome, we all headed for the high school. Once in the school office, we were immediately escorted to an interview office and seated. Within seconds, the vice-principal himself came in, smiled reassuringly and joined us by the desk. After briefly discussing the daughter's problem, we made the request for a home teacher. A secretary was called in, arrangements were quickly made, and the home teacher was assigned to our daughter for as long as needed. Further, the daughter was assured that she could graduate with her class.

The wife never forgot this. She quietly marvelled that such a sticky problem had been solved so smoothly. The home teacher turned out to be a warm-hearted soul, a cheerful matron of the arts, well travelled, and the two got along beautifully. The daughter graduated, a very happy girl indeed!

I remembered the "squares." Somehow, the guides had managed to focus helpful attention on us just when it was needed. Turning to Lenora, I tried to properly thank the guides for their kind, gracious help:

━━━━━

This child was well worth helping. Be gentle with her. She is a free spirit and must learn to spread her wings. She has great potential. She will come into her glory at age twenty two.

━━━━━

One sunny afternoon soon after, Larry asked if he could join me at a session with Lenora. I was delighted and replied, "Glad for the company. Maybe we'll get a chance to try an experiment today." Larry was a quiet soul, known for his dry, pixie sense of humor. Once before, during a group chat concerning rebirth, he had quietly interrupted with the statement that he'd just had a "flashback." When I asked what he meant by this, he had calmly replied, "Well, I just remembered that five hundred years ago, you borrowed twenty dollars from me—and you never paid it back." I'd almost choked with laughter and promised to start paying for Larry's coffee to pay off the debt.

Once again with Lenora, Larry sat quietly as the questions flowed. I first thanked my son's guides for their healing help during Bill's recent leg surgery and hospital confinement. They graciously replied:

━━━━━

There is no need, for this has been accepted and has been given. The duty, the pleasure, the loving is all on our side.

━━━━━

Opening a old book, I displayed several artistic renditions of man's interpenetrating "bodies"—the physical, the astral, the mental, the causal—all rather colorful. We discussed astral travel, then I asked whether man thinks with his 'mental body,' his 'astral body,' or merely with the physical brain while in the waking state. I also asked, "Does each of these 'bodies' have a brain and a mind?"

━━━━━

No. Each contains a segment or section of that which is the total or the "all." Each is related or tied to that which is the "you." You will find that at all of these stages, man is both able to think and to see, to comprehend and to know, but these are on differing planes or levels of his own mind.

━━━━━

"That explains why one can consciously experience while astral living or travelling, and during 'out of body events,' I said. Then, gazing with curiosity at the luminous, colorful auras around the bodies portrayed in the book, I asked, "To Herod and Harold, do we really look like a bunch of colored easter eggs?" (The answer came rather delicately:)

You appear as light to us.

"Do they have patterns? Do our emotions show as patterns?"

The emotions show as colors, and these colors come as patterns, for there is a feeling or a motion or an energy that goes with each ray of color. You will find that these things are best defined to man as patterns in thinking, but to us they come more as a rush, or feeling.

"If we look at this painting, can they see our mental projection?"

Yes . . . the shape, the color, the sound, the feeling is there, and we are aware of that which you are projecting. We are able to define and recognize shape. However, those things which appear to you as shape, many times for us do not have the same definite or defined borders, for the unseen to you is visualized by us. Thus the particular item or article that you are looking at takes on a varied shape for us.

I explained, "That's because of our limited eyesight. They see more levels of energy, so the appearance of objects would be different. And they see the 'essence' of things." A sudden thought caused me to ask, "I wonder if Harold and Herod can see the 'essence' of a man?"

Yes. We are able to see the depths, the purity, the reality, the beauty that is there at all times, even when it is so enmeshed in the muddy surroundings that it is difficult for a

physical eye to see. We are able to see the beauty that is
everpresent.   ●━━●━●━●━●

This answer had come slowly, warmly and thoughtfully. I proceeded slowly: "Does this 'essence' exist as an individualized or
embodied spiritual entity that is of a high order of intelligence in
higher planes?"

Lenora stated, "This says ALWAYS."

"Should humanity, each one of us, become aware of this 'essence?'"

●━━●━●━●━●

Yes. It is necessary that they begin to look upon their own
divinity, so that they will see the need to be doing some-
thing more useful than that which most people do.
●━━●━●━●━●

When I objected that it is hard for man to think of himself as
divine, Lenora thoughtfully mentioned John, verses 30 through
38, wherein Jesus told a group that was about to stone Him for
blasphemy: "In your own law it says that men are gods. So if the
scriptures, which cannot be untrue, speaks of those as gods to
whom the message of God came, do you call it blasphemy when
the One sanctified and sent into the world by the Father says, 'I
am a Son of God?'" (Note—original Greek manuscripts trans-
late "a" Son of God, not "the.")

"In our book, would it be advisable to explain the necessity for
both potentials, good and evil, to exist for growth purposes?"

●━━●━●━●━●

This is essential, *for all must realize the balance and the*
place that each plays in the whole kingdom.
●━━●━●━●━●

"And should we stress the futility of judging either one's self or
another, since everyone is constantly changing and growing?"

●━━●━●━●━●

Ah . . . this is an essential also, for this is one of the main
areas where man works—in a very unconscious level—in a
negative manner.   ●━━●━●━●━●

"Can you advise what level or stratum of society we should
write the book for, or what segment of society might be most receptive?"

Those who walk the earthplane in a very normal manner, with a solid intelligence, are those who need to be tuned to the higher needs of the universe. Once these are implanted with the desire to see a total plan, then much can be accomplished, for those who are from the outer realms are able to work quite rapidly. But the desire must cause the individual to reach upward and outward, to listen, to seek, to find. Only as the desire is implanted can the help be given.

(I had read that seraphic help is ineffective in the absence of magnetic pull of some type. Either faith, belief, knowledge, or loving desire must generate the higher gravity that pulls open the door. I remembered an old saying that my former Spanish teacher was fond of quoting: "The arrow she goes nowhere until the bow she is drawn!")

Then came the experiment. I explained what I had in mind, an idea that came to me during a flight. There used to be a method of synchronizing the propellers on four-engined aircraft. By carefully adjusting the RPM between adjacent propellers, the stroboscopic line, or "shadow," between the propellers could be made to "stop," or stand still. If Herod and Harold would stand adjacent to each other—even though their vibrations were known to be above the speed of light—I hoped to be able to see the "strobe shadow" between them, under proper conditions. When I explained this to Lenora, she appeared interested and asked Herod and Harold.

We are willing to try. . .

With Larry's help, I quickly placed an adjustable mirror outside in the front yard. We turned and canted it so that it reflected a beam of sunlight through the living room window and across the full length of the room. Then we returned and joined Lenora to take up a position where we could scan along the path of the sunbeam. It wasn't long before we detected silvery-blue 'flames' flickering faintly around the beam, about half the distance across the room. Lenora said they were giving her the signal that they were "trying" to adjust their frequencies down to a spectrum that could produce a visible "step-down shadow." Larry squatted down to get a better look and I followed suit. Suddenly I exclaimed, "Say! . . Take a look at that!"

There, right in front of our staring eyes, was a slender, tapering shaft of shining silvery radiance! It was a high vibration indeed, for a "shadow," but it was clearly visible!

After exuberantly thanking Harold and Herod for successfully helping with the experiment, I asked Larry if he might have a question or two to ask. After a moment's thought, he asked a question concerning man's efforts to reach the moon and explore space: "Is this a proper direction at this time, or would we do better to firstly take care of the poor?"

No, mankind must be allowed to reach out, to discover and explore the architecture of his Father-Creator in other systems. He must not be prevented from expanding his own nature. A way will be found to care for the needy simultaneously with man's explorations into space.

The serious problems of family irritations came up, the conflicts and hurts that often afflict well-meaning parents. These caused stresses to both the parents and the children, leaving guilt feelings in their wake.

You must realize that there are many aeons of lifetimes before this one, and you have encountered these same children or personages before. Many times these anxieties have built up in past times, and are only coming to the fore in this particular life. However, you will also fully realize that the "total concept" of love—as you will one day come into it—can be that which erases all of the hurts, the anxieties, the problems. Know that this is what mankind needs to work towards, for as total understanding and love can be given from the birthpoint on, much of the past will be erased or "saved by grace." You will find that this is the way of things to come.

Do not be too harsh on yourselves, nor blame yourself thoroughly, for you also are a product of that which was given to you as a child. You are a product of the thinking of

*your times and the concepts of those schools of thought
that have gone on before your times.*

*We do not judge you. Why judge others so harshly? Be
not so hard on yourselves, nor on others.*

◆━━◆━━◆━━◆━━◆

Thinking of all those past lives, I asked if I had always displayed the same basic personality. Very slowly came the following:

◆━━◆━━◆━━◆

*To a great extent, yes; to the extent that your interest has
always been in the moon and the stars, and the things
away from the earth; to the extent that you have been one
who has always cared greatly about persons and things.
These characteristics have been with you always. The
understanding level has changed exceedingly. The seeing
of beauty in the earth has always been a part of you.*

◆━━◆━━◆━━◆━━◆

Lenora then asked if I had written any more poetry, so I dug
into my notes, pulled forth a scribbled sheet of paper, and recited:

BUBBLES

Gleaming spheres that soar aloft,
        Sunbeams dance on curves so soft;
Splintered scenes of colors bright,
        Entrance the eye, the mind delight.
A primal form, this glowing round,
        It floats with ease in silent sound;
On breeze's wings, with serenity,
        Its beauty grows in eternity.
With curious hand, the mystic child
        Reaches forth to find its core;
The silent burst, with Laughter's smile,
        'Twas there an instant, now no more.
Reflection asks, 'Was not that core
        But part of all the air that Is?
And are we bubbles, ascending high,
        In radiant Light that is really His?'

Lenora once again asked me to be sure and "save the poems." (Usually I throw into 'file X' all my extraneous notes and scraps.) Thinking back, I suddenly recalled Larry's "flashback" and couldn't resist asking, "By the way . . . What does one do with a friend who states that he has just had a 'flashback' and remembers that five hundred years ago, I borrowed twenty dollars from him and never paid it back?"

(On the heels of Larry's embarrassed chuckle and Lenora's delighted laughter, the following advice dryly crept through:)

One asks him, "Where is the receipt?"

I was so unprepared for this witty retort that I chuckled to myself for days. Sitting at home, I began to dream up some humorous questions for Herod and Harold, hoping to relieve the monotony of one serious session after another. The next session (late March, 1972) commenced with the statement:

"The following facetious items are offered for future improvements on this planet: number one, perhaps the seaweed along our coasts might be reduced so that my son and I can go fishing more often?"

(Lenora, smiling:) *. . . How could you have food planted more readily at your doorstep than to have it washed upon your shore? Know that there is much good to be gained from the seaweed. Look to that which it gives, rather than the fish which it hides.*

"Number two: could the orbit of our moon be changed so that we might have twice as many full moons? This would help our wild canine friends to exercise their vocal calls more often, thereby improving their tonal quality, and of course, all the lovers on earth would then have twice the number of opportunities to get romantic."

This is also true: that there are those who go "loony" at this particular time of the month, so it is necessary that they not be exposed to this more often than they have already.

Lenora was dabbing at a tear of laughter as I said that it was probably lucky that we have so few full moons, in the final analysis. Then, number three: "Perhaps the orbit of earth could be re-regulated to exactly 360 days, thereby simplifying calendars, taxes, paychecks, and result in more accurate horoscopes for hopeful ladies?" (Lenora chuckled:)

This is a valid observation. We shall try to accommodate it in our future worlds. Rest assured that your words have been heard this day.

We didn't know what to make of this; perhaps we were being taken seriously. Somewhat less confidently, I gave number four: "Perhaps the sun might 'blink' precisely at noon, which could eliminate the noisy noon lunch whistle, and also, would certainly be a handy aid to navigation?"

This is true. However, recall that the sun would have to move in sudden jerks, for if it were exactly noon in exactly all the places at once, it would be necessary to have a jerky sun.

I now laughed, reassured that they were joking. Funny, thinking of a jerky sun! Then number five: "Perhaps mans' ears might be improved so that a rapid-action valve would close, to prevent eardrum damage when he is exposed to loud, unexpected blasts of noise, like from his wife?"

(Lenora, again chuckling:). . . *This is very true. This would certainly be a remedy to alter that which man has brought upon himself; namely, "hard hearing." You would find that man has learned to cope with these noises, and in thus doing, has tuned out his own hearing ability. It would be well if this could be . . . (pause) . . . plugged in on the outside some way.*

I mentioned earplugs and their beneficial use in noisy areas, then, as a finale, gave my ace recommendation:

"You might try to eliminate the never-ending problems of man's wars and strife by increasing sexual aggression on this planet. Men would be so wearily happy that they would forget wars and dismiss strife as merely blockages to bliss!"

━━━━━━

We had already thought of that, and yet it did not seem to be the answer, for without the strife, there could not be "growth" . . . remember the positive and negative again.

This would be a state of bliss, a state of non-growth, a state of . . . (and this came through with twinkly mirth). . . *sleepyheads!*

━━━━━━

At our April, 1972, session, I recalled that at the commencement of a previous session, the guides had suddenly startled me with:

━━━━━━

Greetings!!!

━━━━━━

So this time, thinking that they might desire some formal courtesy, I opened by saying, "Greetings!" (Lenora promptly added:)

━━━━━━

. . . and salutations to you!

━━━━━━

After some warming preliminaries, I kicked off with a serious question: "What does the 'All' mean, to mortals?"

━━━━━━

The "All" pertains to all mortals on the planet, and yet each within themselves is complete, as a cell within the body is complete within itself. However, it does not function fully nor properly by itself, nor completely cut off and alone. One must remember that although they are individual and total - and important - they are necessary to the total "All."

━━━━━━

"Did God really lose part of Himself so that we can live, exist, and experience?"

And yet did not truly lose, for they are only separated or apart from Him. This is the part which is so anxious to return to the whole, which is so anxious to become a part of the ongoing dream that is that which is the God-Force. Know that man, as a body, only reaches up to encompass this for a time, and releases it each time a little more fullblown than when it first entered the earth experience.

———

"How can we reach this Divine God-Force?"

———

Through the art or schooling of meditation, of learning to quiet self; for there is a great deal which goes on, on the mental and other levels, that are as a constant jumble or confusion. It is extremely difficult for this Divine Spark to come through. The Bible might refer to this as "the still, small voice," or man himself might refer to this in this manner; and even as it is a "still, small voice" or a knowing from within, one must learn to listen and evaluate so that they can tell whether it is the stronger emotional push that is coming forward, or whether it truly is the "still, small voice," the urgings of the Divine Thought Adjuster. Only by learning to go to the deeper levels of the mind— where the silence and peace and quiet are—can one learn to truly listen and then follow through. You will find that in time, when one has learned to do this on a regular basis, they will then be able to be consciously aware that they are following this guidance at all times. It becomes much as an automatic action, such as driving your car. Once you have learned how to use your pedals in conjunction with the gears, it flows.

———

(It was primarily from the above advice that I started Transcendental Meditation™, selecting that method as the easiest and quickest to be found locally. It proved to be brief (twenty minutes), effortless (no contemplation or concentration), so simple that even kids learned to meditate. I did not have to sit in a lotus position, I did not have to quit smoking or change my life

*style, nor did I have to join any dues-paying club. I immediately
began to notice a new sense of enriched vitality, of clarity of
thought, of calm, dynamic poise and purpose. I asked for Herod's
and Harold's opinion of Transcendental Meditation™, and they
answered, "Like skipping from mountaintop to mountaintop . . .
The Royal Road.")*

I asked, "Where is creativity in daily life?"

━━ ━━ ━━ ━━ ━━

*This is the thought of love, the helping hand, the minor
good that you are able to do for yourself, or for another. Do
not feel that this is selfish when it is done for self, but know
that to any degree in which you help to create a better—or
even slightly better—atmosphere or attitude in the areas
around yourself, you will find that this in itself is creative,
for it is helping to lift the total universe. You may be unable
to see this, but if it is seen from the beyond, this is the important point. Know that as enough of those who walk the
earthplane can lift, to even one nth of a degree, their own
environment, they are—as a total race or planet—being
lifted to that same degree, for there are others upon the
planet who are doing the same.*

━━ ━━ ━━ ━━ ━━

"It is not easy to understand why the saying, 'Be ye perfect,
even as the Father in heaven is perfect,' was given on this planet.
How can this apply to mortals who are experimental, limited,
partial, and temporary?"

━━ ━━ ━━ ━━ ━━

*Be always aware that there is a measure of perfection
within you, and that you must live up to that measure of
perfection, however small it might be . . . . . for as each
stage of perfection is reached, you will find that new areas
of perfection open up. Do not dwell on the infirmities . . .
the lacks, those things which are less to be desired, but
dwell on the positive sides, those things which are perfect
within you, and strive to increase in the perfection.* (The
reader might recall their motto: The Highest.)

I smiled as I recalled the time I'd told Bill about the God-Spark. My son had promptly put his hand on his head and wisely said, "Just think! Only three inches from infinity!" I asked, "Is this 'perfection' within us the God-Force, the Absolute Source that we should seek?"

—■—■—■—■—■—

This is the perfection that you can measure against. This is the perfection that can profess itself through you. This is the perfection that is a "Spark" of the "Total." Yes, to your question.

—■—■—■—■—■—

"For those who find vulgarity offensive, how can they avoid this?"

—■—■—■—■—■—

It is not necessary to flinch nor to turn away from such things, but only to send thoughts of "blessings" toward that one. In time, that one may change because of these.

—■—■—■—■—■—

"How is man to cope with those past events of a negative, or wrong nature, that he has committed?"

—■—■—■—■—■—

Man must stop judging himself so harshly, for the evaluations are continually and constantly changing. *This is part of the evolution of* all *areas of life. Stop, evaluate, do not judge, but* move on.

—■—■—■—■—■—

"Still, man has no 'erase button' for his guilts . . ."

—■—■—■—■—■—

The erase button is "forgiveness." For the one who can truly learn the art of forgiveness, you will find that these do not continue after death. For as he truly forgives himself, the grace of God enters his life, and through grace he is forgiven and need not necessarily repay.

—■—■—■—■—■—

"The man with ethics cannot merely whitewash past guilts by saying, 'I forgive myself' . . . He must face reality."

*The key here would be to "let go," to release, to allow.
These are the key words which will help you to advance
without the great effort of rising above, or overcoming.
Know that as you truly forgive yourself and "accept" the
situation where you stand at that particular moment in the
eternity of time, you will find that you are then a new being; new in that you no longer commit the particular sin,
but neither are you totally responsible for that which was
committed in a time before your total enlightenment as of
this moment.*

"During physical life, is man three distinctly separate states
of consciousness: the inner self, the conscious self, and the High
Self?"

*Yes, but they are not cut apart. These three stem from the
same core.*

"Does my High Self consciousness feel what I feel?"

Always. There is a very close attunement here.

"How would you describe my High Self?"

*Keen, sharp . . . very wise . . . a remarkably creative
mind . . . one who is busy, very interested in this course
of progress.*

"Does He have many helpers?"

Many, many . . .

"How does the High Self view us, all the projected personalities?"

*Two way channels to work with and through . . . loves
them all equally.*

"What is His usual demeanor?"

Blissful . . .

"During the 'between life' stages, does procreation ever occur?"

No, there is no particular need, for in the "between life" stage they are totally responsible for themselves and their own growth. They have great areas to work with, great decisions to be made . . .

"Can the High Self, or Soul Being, recall both positive and negative experiences from past lives?"

Yes. It has the ability to retain that which is necessary for future times, so that it will be able to identify without reliving the experience.

"Would not the 'discards' be the day-to-day affairs, those mundane events that we ourselves soon forget?"

They can also be the very painful experiences, or those which have caused a good deal of trauma. For if this has been worked through, it is then a good experience and one which needs to be retained for future use. Also, the daily life is a part of the overall picture. However, it is not recalled instantly . . .

"Then the Soul Being can salvage the 'result' and discard the painful or traumatic event?"

For this is then erased, or neutralized, or equalized . . . "Grace."

"Are Soul Consciousness (High Self) and human consciousness temporarily spaced apart for learning purposes?"

They are two isolated systems which, for convenient's sake, must be separated. However, before the total consciousness can go on into the next phase of learning or knowing, it is necessary that these two be merged. This can be accomplished even at a "between time" level.

"Does one have to merge with one's Soulmate before continuing on into higher realms and more advanced planets?"

No, these two will progress at the same time, but it is not necessary to be "one."

"Just like 'forever buddies' then?" (Their answer reflected amusement:)

Yes.

"Do these twin Soul Beings ever meet here as him-her incarnations . . . here in the physical realm?"

They can, but very, very rarely.

"Must be quite a magnetic 'pull' when they do."

There is too much completion, too much of a feeling of satisfaction, and thus this is not a probable meeting. Those who would find their other half, their true Soulmate, would find that they do not continue to progress nor to grow. There is too much involvement with each other to be of service to mankind.

"What is the 'glow feeling' that flows through me sometimes?"

This is the presence of your Divine Thought Adjuster, who has helped you. This is the presence that you need to harmonize with, to flow with.

"Can you enlighten us with some principles essential to life?"

Freedom of expression . . . not the "right" of expression.

Gratitude for all forces, all acts, all beings, is very necessary, regardless of status or standing. More can be found in The Urantia Book.

We pondered the meanings within the first principle. There seemed to be a subtle difference, a separation between "freedom of expression" and the "right of expression." This might refer to one's rights in relation to the rights of others, but that where one has the right to express, one then has the freedom to express uniquely.

"What could the second principle mean?" I asked Lenora. She replied, "Well, it could mean gratitude for all the supporting forces in nature and appreciation of all the patient guides who assist and love us, and also, for all those who counsel, teach, and guard over this planet." Wondering, I impulsively asked, "Are you perfect beings?" (The droll answer returned:)

Well . . . almost.

Amidst chuckles, we bid a fond farewell to Herod and Harold and ended the session. I again assured Lenora that the information seemed excellent and highly informative. Our only problem in the future would be writing a manuscript that might prove suitable for publication.

The hot spring sun blazed down through a serene blue sky over the race-track. A perfect May day had dawned for the Alfa Club's semi-annual driving instruction event. Being non-profit, the club's dues structure—plus a very modest entry fee—had supplied the funds to rent the track, buy insurance, and hire an ambulance crew for safety. More than thirty privately owned Alfa Romeo's had been thoroughly inspected by race mechanics. The car owners had been briefed on track safety rules, safety signals, and the specific hours of class instruction. Three groups of instructors were assigned specific student-drivers, to teach them the fine art of smooth, safe, highspeed driving in their own cars. I was assigned three beginners.

My family was a solid group of Alfa enthusiasts. Our daughter Karen, her husband Al, and son Bill were on tap for this event, even though Bill was below the permissible driving age and could not participate. All morning, Bill could be seen walking about, photographing the sleek, shining Alfa's, occasionally borrowing my helmet and cadging rides with other drivers.

During the lunch break, Bill asked if he might ride with me in Betsy. Perhaps for just a couple of laps? (He well knew that I would give in and demonstrate some intermediate driving techniques.) Smiling, I borrowed a helmet for Bill, strapped him in with the seatbelts, then warmed her up. As we idled out onto the track, the temperature readings began to rise and I waited patiently until they reached the normal range. Then I shifted into an attitude of calm but determined "go." Precisely skimming the razor-edges at the inside apex of the turns, I quietly lectured Bill. "See how we brake at this point . . . then we downshift like thus . . . then, coming into the turn, we get on it right here and use Betsy's power to pull us through the turn. See how we come out into the straightaway at a faster speed?" Bill sat quietly absorbing every detail as I increased our speed.

Neither of us was aware that Bill's sister and her husband had hiked out to a far turn, hoping to snap a photo of Betsy in action. Betsy's paint color was a lustrous Italian red which, together with classic, shining trim, photographed well. But as fate would have it, they snapped the shutter at the exact instant the accident happened.

It was during the third lap, while approaching a highspeed turn, that my attention was diverted. Betsy's speed was a bit high for the turn. As I reached for the gearshift knob to downshift, my scan-vision flickered toward two familiar figures standing beside the curve. While my attention was fleetingly divided, I downshifted too soon. The action was automatic, but the results were disastrous! The engine screamed and the tach needle leaped off the scale past the 8000 mark. A metalic clattering sound followed by dense billowing oil-smoke out the rear, together told the sad tale. "Dag-nabit!" I groaned. "Now I've done it! . . . Scattered that beautiful engine but good!" Bill looked perturbed, asking faintly, "What happened, Dad?" Shaking my head curtly, I said, "Well, I over-revved the engine, but don't worry. We'll get Betsy back to the pits and bum a ride home with someone else."

Idling back around the track, the engine rattled like it had swallowed a valve or broken a piston. We parked in the pit area and walked off. A bystander and the club president inquired about the oil-smoke on the track, but I didn't want to discuss it. After a mild comment, Bill and I joined another group and I returned to my instructing. Strangely, my concentration was such that day that I completely forgot the previous incident.

About four that afternoon, a student got a flat tire. He'd brought along so much gear that he'd not been able to fit his spare tire into the trunk. I quickly offered to drive him to a service station where he could get it repaired. Throwing the flat tire into Betsy's trunk, we drove two miles to the station and waited patiently until it was patched and refilled with air. It was after five when we returned, and nearly everyone had departed. Helping the student replace the wheel, making sure it would hold its pressure, Bill and I then loaded up our supplies and departed. The heat of the day had tired us out. We leisurely joined the freeway traffic and loafed along, sharing comments about the different Alfa's, the strange roar of Alfa engines—a sound not unlike that of singing hornets—and how great a day it had been for all.

Suddenly Bill turned around and gazed through the rear window with a strange look on his face. I smiled and asked, "What's behind us, the fuzz?" Bill said, "No, that's the funny part of it . . . There's nothing behind us, not even oil-smoke!" I looked at him, puzzled. My mind was blank. "What are you getting at?" Bill protested, "But Dad! . . . Didn't we have an accident? . . . Don't you remember, back on the track, when Betsy's engine screamed?"

My mind jumped! Like striking lightning, the vivid memory flashed into focus. I listened carefully to the engine . . . It sounded normal! Gently I added power, cautiously listening for any rattles in the engine. Betsy seemed perfectly smooth in each of the five gear ratios! "Well," I said softly, "I'm not going to question this one. Somebody up there sure did us a big favor, though. An engine overhaul is pretty expensive." We relaxed and smiled, enjoying the secure feelings of a day well spent, some remarkable experiences, and a safe ride home. We never forgot though.

It was two months later that the family eagerly scanned some of the snapshots taken up at the race track. One, in color, showed a little red Alfa approaching a turn with oil smoke starting to pour out of her tail-end.

And two years later, at the Alfa West Shop, Betsy's engine was tested and given a valve job. There were no broken parts. That day at the track must have been a day of special "Grace."

Chapter VIII
The Unchangeable Symbol (?)

The problem came up just as I was reaching for a deeper understanding of one of the 'principles.' Instead of putting down my notes and listening, I tried to continue studying and pay attention to my wife at the same time. Within a few minutes, we found ourselves in a heated argument that soon escalated into a rare spat! Angry, I slept on the couch and left early the next morning for work.

When I returned, she mentioned that the house had been without heat since I'd left. Raising an eyebrow, I searched for the problem and there, inside the furnace, I found a totally burned up blower motor. I couldn't believe this! Just one year previously, new air-conditioning had been added and the experts had installed a new two-stage, heavy horsepower motor. Also, I had carefully oiled the motor bearings per specifications.

There was nothing to do but purchase a new (expensive) motor and install it myself. Then I sat down to think over the possible "causes" of such an undesirable "effect." I pondered, "Burned up motor . . . heat . . . resulting in a loss of heat . . . or coldness. Burned up . . . emotionally burned up . . . Oh, oh! The spat!!! So that's what probably caused it! Subtle, subtle, subtle, these little 'lessons' . . . ."

Gradually I became more aware of these "accidents" around me. One hot day down at the stables, a heated argument was overheard out behind one of the barns. Two young people in the heated throes of a divorce were really going at it. I immediately left the vicinity and found something else to do. When Jack, the owner, returned, I remarked that the young couple might do well to 'cool it' before one of them got hurt. I mentioned the furnace motor event.

One week later we received news that the divorcing husband had been involved in a car accident and now lay in the hospital. But when he regained his health, the two continued to fight. Then, in August, 1972, this same man was unexpectedly bitten in the face by his favorite horse. The eventual cost of repairing the results of this 'accident' exceeded eight hundred dollars. The site of his injury? His mouth.

I began to wonder about "school lessons" that no one seemed aware of, that few people could believe. How could humanity learn when we can neither see nor measure emotional forces? People readily accept unseen television and radio waves, but emotional waves?

I knew that I would never have believed such a thing, had it not been for the revealing statements of Harold and Herod. It was rapidly becoming obvious to me that humanity simply could not afford the luxury of blasting out with wrath at some irritation, without reaping a crop of "negative waves" right back where it hurts!

At the start of our next session together, I politely commenced with an expectant, "Greetings!" Nothing happened. Lenora sat there as quiet as a mouse. After an awkward pause, she inquired, "Were you waiting for something?" "Well, I'd sure like to find out if someone's there!", I replied. (Surprise, chagrin, and disbelief reflected through her voice as they stated:)

A-L-W-A-Y-S! . . . . . *your doubt is beyond belief!*

I chuckled to myself, "Boy, they're there alright, but how's a feller to know?" Then I knuckled down and asked, "What can be given to others to awaken them to the dangerous habit of venting wrathful thoughts and feelings? How can they become convinced that this is dangerous?"

●●━━●●━━●●

Tell them to spew forth on a hot frying pan, for th
see that as the bubbles of water spew back at them,
can then envision those things which become "thought-
forms." For as they send these out into space, they will
bounce back with the same impetus that they have gone
forth, just as surely as the words or thoughts have been
spoken or thought. It would be well for those to become
aware of such things as "auras," for they would then be
able to see with their visual eyes those things which are
around others in their thought areas. It is also well if they
feel within themselves the "emotion" that is brought forth
by this anger or wrath, for as they feel this churning or
burning within them, they will have some vague idea of
the intensity of it, and the venom in it.

Each one could begin an experiment that they would be
able to see the "boomerang" effect of these thoughts, for if
they will carefully chart their thought and emotion pat-
terns, they will find that life around them has the same
pattern—in a reflected manner—as that which has gone
forth.

●●━━●●━━●●

"What 'benefits' do people receive from turning away from
negatives toward the positives, the more friendly, helpful aspects of living?"

●●━━●●━━●●

You will find that the same multiplying power or quick
reaction will also come from the positive actions. You will
find that as you give friendship to one person, they may or
may not return it. This is not the implication, but the fact
that you have given, and thus you are open for more
things to come unto yourself. It may come as the return of
a better job, a new opportunity. Even then, it may come in
what appears to be a negative manner. For instance, if
your job is taken from you, you would feel, "there I have
received evil for the fact that I have given good," and yet
within a few short days you may discover that you have
"found" an even better job, or have been encouraged to
move to an area where the opportunities are greater. You
must not try to react immediately to those things which
happen, but only be aware that each thing—when you have

*learned to release totally— can only come to you for a
"good" purpose if you are sending out "good" or positive
actions.*

*You will find that when you can "detach" yourself—gain
the long view or observe from a distance—you will find that
all things begin to fit into a pattern. They may not appear
to be connected—such as your work, your home life, your
spiritual life—these things may appear to be as three separate entities to you, and yet you will find that they have the
interplay that is necessary to bring about the total
"whole," or good for you. Watch, wait, listen, evaluate—
even as you have evaluated the negative things that have
gone forth from you—and you will soon begin to see the
pattern come forth.* ━━━━━

Lenora said that this might explain why "good luck" seemed to
follow those who were genuinely friendly, helpful, and positive.

"What can each person do, in daily life, to best help the
advancement of all life on this planet?" ━━━━━

*The main thing that all can do is to send out a leveling
influence through their constant vigilance of thought. This
need not be a guarded thing, and yet it needs to be one
which is of a constructive nature. If one finds himself beginning to think negatively, or to enlarge upon such things
as war or rape or murder—if these become the central focal
point within their thoughts—then they need to divert their
attention to things which are more helpful . . . unless
there is the knowledge that there is an actual action that
they can take to help minimize these things. Know that
when there is not a physical action that can be taken, then
one must work from the mental plane. And even as you lift
your own vibration or thought to a more positive level, so
you will be helping your fellow man—though he lives in the
next house, the next state, or the next country.*

*Be aware that as each one thinks in a constructive man-
ner, constructive ideas will come toward him, and though
they may not appear to help the particular problem at
hand, they will find that they are able to lay the*

groundwork for future help, or to eliminate future problems.

Thus as one reads the paper or hears the news, or has a reaction to their own immediate family, so they must open their eyes and ears and allow the more constructive ideas and mannerisms to come toward them, and they in turn will release this into the atmospheres to be used by all.

━━━━━

As the weeks sailed by, we began to see this "school" in a new light. All these 'lessons' were not idle, but for purpose. Glancing at the latest statistics on sun energies, we could see that vast amounts of power were not being casually used up for the fun of it, but for humanity to be given time to learn better control over the mental, emotional, and physical areas of life. We were staggered by the statistics, the tremendous amounts of energy being consumed by our solar furnace every second of time. We learned that *564 million tons* of hydrogen fuel are fed each second into the sun's nuclear furnace. This fuel produces 560 million tons of helium and the process of nuclear fusion converts 4 million tons of the material into radiant solar energy. This consumption (per second) amounts to more than 14 billion tons per hour and 345 *billions of tons each day.*

Rather bogged down with the above figures, I asked if the expansion of universes, the infinite details of building towards perfection, might be considered a weighty and absorbing process? An interesting answer came back.

━━━━━

This is well to remember, but also remember that as the workers move along their projected jobs, it is necessary that they sing and have time for mirth, for only through this can they do their best work.

Those who are weighted by the intensity of their jobs will find that they fail through tenseness, rather than through lack of concentration. It is necessary that all things be played into the workman's day, so that the "total picture" can be one of joy, of happiness, of beauty, and of serenity, that harmony—which is so necessary—might also be incorporated into the building materials.

━━━━━

"Why is there so little progress from life to life? One would think that compassion and understanding would be far more prevalent."

●━●━●━●━●

Not necessarily, for you will find that there is a great deal of ability that is carried over. However, each lifetime it must be retriggered so that the "opening" or the awareness of it comes forward. You will also find that the awareness of the "weaknesses" is stronger, and thus, although each person has progressed, they are more aware of their weaknesses than they had been in previous mortal lives.

●━●━●━●━●

I asked Lenora if she might be receptive to another 'experiment.' She glanced upward, shook her head, so I smiled and explained, "No, this is not anything scientific, merely mental. There may be a way to determine just how Harold and Herod 'see' things. Here's how it goes: I'll mentally project some object—or some picture of a physical object—and perhaps we can compare it with whatever they send back into your mind . . . OK?" Lenora asked, "Are you going to tell me what it is beforehand?" "Nope," I said.

Interested, she nodded her head in agreement, so I shut my eyes and concentrated on visualizing the color-image of a tall mountain. Then I added a beautiful castle on its top, with banners waving from its spires and turrets. I held this scene for several seconds and Lenora announced, "They're showing me a 'triangle,' and it has a big shining diamond growing out of its top!"

I sulked gloomily, "Well, that one was a bust! Let's try again." This time I closed my eyes and pictured a lonely seagull flying along an overcast coastal beach, towards evening. Seconds later, Lenora announced that they were showing her a lonesome little child, swaying and playing with a hoola-hoop that went around and around her waist. Again I shook my head, saying that I thought they were way off base. She mentioned she felt the point of the hoola-hoop was that it "stayed up with no visible means of support." I immediately caught the connection: "It stayed up, (so did the seagull), with no visible means of support." But why had Harold and Herod changed it? A lonely little *bird* . . . a lone-

some little *child*! And then I recalled a long ago answer . . .
"Even the animals have a soul." To seraphic minds, as long as it
had a *soul*, it was a *child*! So this was the 'lesson' they were hoping to get across! Lenora and I marvelled at the subtle wisdom
displayed by these seraphim, using my own experiment to open
our understanding!

Then we tackled the 'first answer,' the triangle with the
diamond growing out of its top. I said, "Well, if we were to
analyze a mountain geometrically, it has a base-line and two slop-
ing sides, so perhaps to their eyes it appears as a 'triangle,' but
what could be the meaning of the diamond?" Lenora asked,
"What did you project?" I quickly described the castle on top of
the mountain. With a sudden burst of inspiration (or sheer
genius), Lenora unravelled the mystery-symbols with, "They
must mean a "rock-like" or "gem-like" form of construction on
the mountaintop! The diamond is a "cut stone" and castles are
built out of cut stones! Also, since it is glowing, this indicates
"life" in the diamond and the castle!"

I just sat still and shook my head. What minds! I felt a twinge
of inferiority for a second; then my ego roused itself. Forgetting
that they could read every thought in my head, if they chose, I
began to muse to myself silently, "Foxy, foxy! . . . Well, old
Dad might just save the day yet! We'll just have to come up with
a symbol so unique, so perfect, that there will be no way for
them to 'change' it. Now let's see . . . what could I pick?" Rang-
ing over many possible choices, I discarded each one as a way
was perceived to change it to another meaning. Then I got sharp!

Projecting my mind's vision way, way out to galactic heights, I
gazed back at our tiny dust-mote of a planet. I thought deeply,
"What is the one, single, galactic symbol that distinguishes our
planet from all the millions of her sister planets? Ah! . . . Und
now ve hit der jackpot!!!" To Lenora, I stated, "I know one symbol they can't change! Let's try it one more time and see what we
get!" She looked eagerly expectant as I firmly closed my eyes.
Slowly, carefully, my mind formed the sacred image of an old,
weathered Cross standing forlornly on a deserted hilltop. To my
utter amazement, Lenora almost instantly stated that they were
showing her something of a very unusual design. It was a re-
splendent, glowing "Golden Crown"!

When the shock wore off, I leaned back and purred like a big cat. Now I was finally and supremely certain that Harold and Herod had surely seen my mental projections. There could be no doubt. In the same thought, I silently vowed to never again 'fence' with those brilliant seraphim! I knew that I'd lost the tournament, shot down in flames. I'd done my very best to select an "unchangeable symbol," had gone to galactic heights to find a timeless, planetary symbol. But the seraphim had gone 'higher,' even to Universal heights, and had indeed 'changed' the symbol in a most perfect way!

I had given them the Cross, and their *precisely correct answer* had been "The golden crown of universe sovereignty" that He had earned from that historic, universally stunning ordeal on the Cross. Herod and Harold had pointed an unerring celestial finger at the records of universal history.

As my appreciation for such keen intellects deepened, I probed even farther than I'd intended. Casting aside my notes, I asked, "Why were six differently colored races of man produced on this planet, rather than one?"

●●●●●●

There is a diversity of need even in the souls that come to these particular bodies. You will find that this goes back to the beginnings, because there has always been separation and division, there has always been the special or the individual. Even as God is a "Total," he is as individualized as those souls which come upon the earth. This is the reason that none can understand that from which the soul flows forth.

These six races indicate the varied needs within man, and yet you will find that man, of his own choosing, sends his soul back and forth among these different races, that he might experience the different areas. In the total end, however, they do revert to the origin of that which they chose in the beginning.

●●●●●●

Plunging deeper, I asked, "In order to experience the process of 'growth toward perfection'—rather than creating instant perfection—did the Creator first envision the 'field' in which this process could take place, *before* it could happen?"

True. You are delving into a subject that is extremely difficult to define in earth terms, for there has been such a great involvement in minute detail, in more than envisioning the finished product, in more than creating each particle . . . (A long, thoughtful pause ensued, then:)

It was as though . . . the force . . . which is the life . . . blossomed . . . and is continuing to blossom, or bloom . . . which means that life is continually forcing upward and outward, that all things are continuing in a forward manner, and the older or unused portions are dropping away. This would be considered evolvement. However, know that the force which does this is not an outside force, but more as the sap within the plant which rushes forth, and upward and outward.

●●●●●

I said, "Now that's beautiful! It's not an outside force working on evolution; it's working within it, or 'interpenetrating,' I should guess."

●●●●●

This is an even greater description, for the force is, and was, and has been, and shall be, but it is within and interpenetrating all things, even as you have said.

●●●●●

And further, "Please define for us your term, 'Total Concept' . . ."

●●●●●

This Total Concept, as we speak of it, is something that has not yet been able to be totally lived on the earthplane, for there are too many blocks, too many immunities that are yet being utilized.

Be aware that this "Total Concept" will be when there is an acceptance of all souls on their level, feeling not the slightest remorse that one might not appear to have the mental capabilities of another, not the slightest bit of remorse for a day, or a minute, or an hour that has passed, for a deed not accomplished, for a purpose not completed. It will be a time of existence in love for the "moment." This will be when mankind learns to live in the eternal "now," without a prospect of the morrow nor a worrying about it,

*without a feeling of regret over the past, or even moments
which have passed earlier.*

━ ━ ━ ━ ━

"Will strife and growth have ceased then?"

━ ━ ━ ━ ━

*It will be the healing period for this planet. It will be the
time when all past hurts and karmas are totally healed, and
it will be a time on the earth that the existence will be "perfection." It will be a time when the purpose of this particular place is completed, or finished.*

━ ━ ━ ━ ━

That just about wrapped it up, or so I thought. All that was
needed now was a message from the seraphim to humanity.
Perhaps one more session, before Lenora moved away, would
complete my search. I felt a deep sense of impending loss, that
her family situation required their departure from the area (and
with Lenora went Herod and Harold); but I'd kicked around long
enough to know that all good things must come to an end. I
would have my tapes to listen to, to study for the rest of my life;
and my books . . . There was one puzzling conflict in terms to
solve, though.

Chapter IX

The Multiplex Key

What to think? Months of tape studies had convinced me that Harold and Herod were presenting the facts—concerning karmic debts and consecutive life cycles—as they perceived them, yet Seth (validated through Lenora) had repeatedly stated that all one's lives are lived simultaneously. How could both these opposing viewpoints be correct? I seriously concentrated:

"If *one whole identity* is living *all* its lives *simultaneously,* then the *consciousness* of that identity would have to *divide* itself, or *micro-pulse between each life.*" Then in one mind-opening flash of realization, I found a "key" to rebirth: *the time-sharing operation known as "Multiplex."*

This key can be easily understood by those familiar with radio communications or telephone circuitry. Multiplex is the method used to carry many simultaneous telephone calls along *one wire.* For example, if thirty people in New York were to simultaneously telephone thirty different people in San Francisco, these thirty separate calls are carried on *one wire* between the city centrals. How is this done? The phone company merely *divides time into micro-seconds* and *assigns a different micro-second sequence to each caller.* The whole process is so incredibly fast that each calls seems quite continuous.

Having learned previously that a person's consciousness pulses from cell to cell in the brain—forming thought processes—we could easily accept the possibility of Soul Consciousness dividing into micro-pulsations, then assigning a different micro-pulsed sequence to each mortal life, much like the phone call illustration. The process would be so subtly rapid that each life would seem to be quite individual, separate, and uninterrupted.

When Herod and Harold were asked the question: "Is the process of 'micro-pulsing' used by higher beings to 'multiply' themselves?", they said:

Yes. You will find that the variations from this are minor.

With this in mind, one can visualize a wide "history map" on a wall. The *beginnings* of history on this planet are at the left edge of the map, the *end* of planetary history at the right edge. A 'Soul-being' approaches and deeply analyzes all phases of history, from "left" to "right." It then selects a number of "time-slots" in which to live and experience. By the process of "multiplexing" Its consciousness, It can then project separate channels into *all* Its selected lives simultaneously. Each newborn infant gets one micro-sequenced channel of the Soul-being's Total Consciousness, and as each infant grows throughout life's experiences, so grows the Total Being. One might note that each infant does not receive a "slice" of the whole pie (Soul-being's Consciousness) but *is* (in this analogy) *that Soul-being Itself.* The 'separation' is merely apparent. Micro-pulsing requires that each person *is* the Soul-being. All multiplexed signals are merely "projections" of the main "carrier" beam, are extensions of the *real carrier wave.*

The evidence supporting such a postulate stems from the fact that one can often hear "other" telephone conversations in the distant background during long distance calls. This is caused by improper multiplex operations and various other electronic faults. Likewise, many people have experienced *deja vu,* defined by *Webster's New International Dictionary* as: (F.) Literally, already seen. The experience of "just knowing I've seen this before," (when one also knows that the particular place has never been visited), is a common occurrence among well-travelled people. The cause? Similar to the well-known "cross-talk" between long distance phone calls, *deja vu* could be "cross-experience" between lives—lives that are being lived simultaneously much like those thirty phone calls.

To grasp this concept more easily, one might pick up a "comb." The solid handle portion can represent the Soul-being. Each of the projecting teeth can represent one life in a physical body on the earthplane. The Soul-being sees the comb as a "unity," since It can view the whole comb from broadside. But each human personality has been projected out onto the "tip" of one of those teeth, and therefore must view the teeth in "front" of its position as future lives and those teeth "behind" its position as past lives.

Another example is the television set. Your TV antenna is constantly receiving *all* signals from *all* TV broadcast stations in your area. Yet each television set can display only one channel at a time. (If it doesn't, it needs fixing!) Your channel selector is designed to accept certain bands of frequencies called 'channels.' Within your set, electronic filters are utilized to "screen out" all frequencies outside the particular band, or channel, that you have selected. These ensure channel separation.

In much the same way, the physical brain circuitry seems to "screen out" all other mental frequencies in the thought-spectrum. (Otherwise, there could be no individual thinking. Each brain utilizes its own individual 'channel.')

ESP research is attempting to locate the "channel selector knob" so that "mind to mind," or telepathic communications can take place at will. This is precisely what Lenora seems to have accomplished. Over the years, she has developed a method of "shifting channels," and the resulting communications with those in other planes are self-evident in this book. It is true that this mental shift seems more like switching from television's VHF to the UHF band, but this is essentially no different than switching channels. It dawns here that the physical brain and its nervous system are the limiting factors on the indwelling consciousness of each person. However, there are known ways to refine these systems. How? As has already been stated: *ef-fortlessly*. One simple method is Transcendental Meditation™. There is extensive evidence (available gratis from any SIMS or IMS Center throughout the country), that TM spontaneously produces psycho-biological refinements and improvments to the nervous system, the brain, the personality, to the whole person.

At our next session, October 1972, the questioning resumed with, "I'm curious . . . Can we think of the Divine Thought Adjuster as the High Self, or is It "above" that level; either the Ku, Kane, or Kanaloa?"

━ ■ ■ ■ ■ ●

The Divine Thought Adjuster, as spoken of in **The Urantia Book,** *is that which is of the Higher Selves, that which is above the High Self of the human.*

━ ■ ■ ■ ■ ●

Lenora added: "It seems to be the one in the middle." I asked, "Perhaps the Kane?" Lenora replied in the affirmative. Continuing, I asked, "The 'Soul,' then is the Whole Self?" She answered, "Yes, more nearly." "Seth, then, is something higher than the Soul?"

━ ■ ■ ■ ■ ●

Seth, in combination with the Highest Self that you can understand at this point in the physical, is the culmination which would be known as a Soul.

━ ■ ■ ■ ■ ●

"How are you able to transition between all these different energy-planes?"

━ ■ ■ ■ ■ ●

Our frequencies are variable as is necessary, for there are times when they need to be of higher valuation and times when they can be lowered. We have a framework that we work within.

━ ■ ■ ■ ■ ●

"When you are in transit between solar systems, how do you maintain communications contact with your Center?"

━ ■ ■ ■ ■ ●

By thought contact.

"Do Time and Space exist only below the speed of light?"

— — — — —

Time is only a measurement for the mind, for that which needs to have a basis of operation, a point of context. Yes, you are correct in knowing that it is not necessary, nor a part of that which is beyond the speed of light, for this again is only a measurement of time and space.

— — — — —

"You once stated that each cell of the body has its own consciousness. Is this a consciousness "of" . . . or "as" the whole body?"

— — — — —

As the whole body. It realizes its own function, its own part. It realizes a need and the desire to fulfill, thus it becomes that which is necessary to the whole.

— — — — —

"What can be given as to our inability to 'know' the Whole Self?"

— — — — —

The part that needs to be given there is the fact that man must realize he is only a vehicle for a part of a total race, that he is only one speck of awareness within even those parts which are "himself," and that "this" is just a speck of that which is the "total being," and on and on it goes. However, he must not be bogged down with the immensity or enormity of it all, but to know that he is very vital and essential, even as each cell is essential to the body . . . "

— — — — —

"What percentage of the Whole Self is man's conscious mind?"

— — — — —

Three hundredths of one percent . . . much as the tip of an iceberg.

— — — — —

"What factors should be considered when searching for 'self-worth?'"

— — — — —

The main factor to consider is the fact that one is "life," and life is "all." Life and love are one, and these manifest as a "being." It is necessary to consider this to the nth degree, that you might be aware that there is an Intelligence that cares. This in itself makes man of the highest order. To become even greater within that same structure, he will strive to fulfill his mission and to co-operate with the power that is.

Man is greatly blessed and is keenly developed. He must know these things that he can then begin to see his other areas of emotional response, physical response, etcetera, in their own light and in their own balanced place; that he might not consider one particular area of flaw as a "total" lack of worth, but say, "Ah, yes . . . I see this is an area that needs to be considered or worked with, to bring the total into balance." Man needs to know that he Is.

━━━━━

"This merging of consciousness into the physical body has been done so cleverly, so firmly and neatly, that it is hard to imagine each man discovering all these things on his own. Is it not more likely that man must be 'taught' these things?"

━━━━━

Man knows, in the "reality" of self, that these are true and so. It is not possible for each man to discover this on his own, nor to reach a stage where he can evolve, for this would take too great a period of "time." It is necessary that those who have the ability, the knowledge, "bring" this to the earth so that it can be delved into by those who have already been seeking to evolve. You will find that it is necessary that teachers come to man, and yet man must also reach upward to receive this. It is not of his own evolving that it comes forth. Wisdom, without the desire to learn, is wasted. This is why the preparations have been so long, so thorough.

━━━━━

"Is one of the goals to subdue and control all desires?"

━━━━━

Only those which are a hindrance, only those which would hold one back to the earth . . . the desires of "love," "selfworth," or "recognition of the God-force" are not subdued. *There are many areas of life that are not sub-dued, but those things which are more of the physical plane need to be "controlled."*

━━━━━

"It wouldn't do, then, to stare at all the pretty girls?"

━━━━━

Why not? This is one of the ways in which man can be-come more beautiful himself, by observing those more beautiful creations around him.

━━━━━

I then brought up the subject of karmic debts, in the sense of "As ye sow, so shall ye reap," by asking, "Where is the justice in the case of two hypothetical men, one of whom feels no guilt whatsoever when committing hurtful acts; the other (a more ethically evolved man), feels the guilt and thereby reaps nega-tive karma; yet both acts were identical?"

━━━━━

Recall that he who does not feel the guilt—though he is not aware of a reprisal in this lifetime—yet is this within his consciousness and he will have to reap that which he has sown at another time.

Know that though you do not see "those who live by the sword" necessarily "die by the sword," neither do you see those who have not reaped the debt of consciousness have to pay the price that is there . . . for they will reap this, though it be in another lifetime, and it may be triple the debt that they had yet incurred.

━━━━━

(I pondered, "Triple the debt," and thought, "Their sense of justice seems to follow their motto alright!") I said, "Then there must be different levels of justice, because we know that an act considered by a past society to be "good" is many times consid-ered "bad" by a later society, and vice versa."

━━━━━

It is so . . . and you will recall that many of the things with which you are now dealing are on the physcial plane, and these are the things which are governed by the earth-laws of the time. You will also realize . . .

(Unfortunately, Lenora's doorbell rang at this point, interrupting Herod and Harold. After a short break, we continued along the same line of probing:)

"Then it wouldn't work to use the justice system of some other planet, or some other 'time.' One must keep justice within one's own sphere?"

———————

This is the basic truth that you are now reaching. You are aware that many things are unjust as far as the earthman can visualize, and yet recall that there is a far greater." . . . (evidently meaning a greater perspective).

You yourself have spoken of billions and billions of aeons, and thus you must realize that many of the things which appear to be very important to mankind at this time are of minor consequence in the total picture.

Be not so hard on yourselves, nor on others. Know that there is a time of justice. Know also that there are many things which are in the physical realm that are unjust, and yet these are those areas that shall be worked out in the aeons ahead.

———————

I commented, "Trust in Allah but be sure to tie your camel!" Then I turned a page and asked, "Is the reason that the Teachers and Prophets of old would not cohabit with women due to a belief that they would, by doing so, lose their psychic powers?"

———————

No. It was mainly because the taking on of added responsibilities could only detract from their mission, that of moving from place to place frequently so as to spread the teachings and light of knowledge among many. Know that this loss of energy, if there is love—even one iota of love—can be replenished. It is not lost.

———————

"Can we clarify a confusing point? Is the 'soul' actually the inner self?"

———————

No. This inner self is that which is contained and is progressing, is continuing to evolve. The soul is that which is adjacent to or beyond the immediate mind level; and yet is not held back by it, but is an accumulation of all the thought-minds that have been a particular part of that soul.

———————

"That latter sounds like the Whole Self, doesn't it? . . . I wonder if they can describe my inner self."

———————

She . . . overshadowed he . . . there are two facets to this which is within you, but the female side is more dominant and this is the creative, beauty aspect of your self. This is the understanding, the comprehension, the compassion, and the ability to "see through" (concepts), that is you.

———————

"Is this inner level of consciousness evolving to become more like my waking state of consciousness?"

———————

Continually. To feel, to think, to act, to rationalize, to do all things as you would do. Thus you become as its teacher. It is essential that you master yourself, that you might help this level master itself.

———————

"Are we evolving to become High Selves?"

———————

You are supposed to be continually evolving your "selves," for only as you pull one up, are you able to also push another one on; for each in turn becomes as the teacher of that which is one step lower. Know that you have the ability to become gods in time, for this is the eventual evolution of mankind as made within the image of God.

———————

At the time, such a statement could only bring me right out of my chair. In the back of my mind, I'd been pondering the frailties of human nature—the ignorance, the injustices, the pathetic attempts of man to uphold high ideals, the distorted beliefs— and the thought of such creatures becoming 'gods' was beyond my comprehension. I firmly stated, "It is *exceedingly difficult* for the mind of man to conceive of ever becoming a 'god.' (The response was rather firmly stated also:)

Why is this so difficult to believe when you know *the extreme power and energy that is poured forth from the many sources at one time? Know that these things* are *possible or they would not have been stated. There is no great problem here, only* time, time, time. *So be patient and know that these things* do *happen,* have *happened, and* can happen.

As man begins to recognize his own abilities, this is only when he begins to awaken from the long, deep slumber that he has been in for the aeons of time. As he wakens from this slumber, he begins to play with his mind and work with it in ways that may appear to be devious, or angry, or hurtful. As he begins to realize the strength of this particular energy, he then begins to try to develop or discipline it. As this discipline becomes more firm, the reaction takes place so that the energy is formed into a particular use, or vessel. Then it becomes more useable, and from that point on, it can become more godlike . . . . these are in relative terms, for "God"—as man uses the term—is not the ultimate. "God" is only the beginning of that which has left the physical.

▬▬▬▬▬

"What good would it do to write a book with such farsighted concepts in it, if only a handful of open-minded people will believe it?"

▬▬▬▬▬

It is not lost in the consciousness of "total man." Know that this is the way in which the help is being implanted. It is being given and regiven in many, many forms at this time. It is to be charged and discharged to those who will listen, whether they hear with their ears or not. It is going into their consciousness and this shall again, in time, repeat to the point that those who come upon the earth in future days will have this knowledge born innately within them, and not have to reach to the times past nor into the outer realms to receive it.

▬▬▬▬▬

Thinking of those people who really needed help, I tried to formulate broad questions that might elicit some enlightening answers:

"What can be told those who feel that they are not progressing?"

━━ ━━ ━━ ━━ ━━

They again need to be made aware of the fact that they are seeing a very minor facet of that which is the "Soul" of themselves. They need to know that they are progressing many times, whether they are aware of it or not; and whenever they are "wasting time," they are not progressing, but they are not regressing. They need to know that they can hold one area for a certain length of time, and then they will feel an impatience or unsettledness within, which will cause them to again seek and search. They need to realize that although the progress is not perceptible in their eyes, the very fact that they are learning anything, whether it be patience, maturity, love, and desire, this in itself is what is necessary to the total, so that this is not wasted.

━━ ━━ ━━ ━━ ━━

"What can be told those who feel guilty over past mistakes?"

━━ ━━ ━━ ━━ ━━

All they can be told is to keep forward on the path, much as one who regresses on a diet. They must know that they cannot be guilty over those things which have gone before, but only pick up their burden and continue forward with that which they know to be right or true. You can only tell those who have made a mistake that this is the manner in which they have learned, and that to repeat the mistake is then the sin—but not to have committed the mistake. Knowing that as one learns through a heartfelt lesson, they are then more firmly entrenched in those things which they know to be right and correct.

Be patient with them, and teach them also to be patient with themselves, for if they become impatient over a past mistake, they are then encouraging another fault to come forth, the fault of impatience.

━━ ━━ ━━ ━━ ━━

I asked, "Why is it necessary to actually experience the traumas that so many endure? Can we not learn by carefully observing others?"

●━●━●━●━●

*Only he who has been in the totally drunken state can truly
lend a helping hand of compassion to his brother who lies
in the gutter.*   ●━●━●━●━●

"What can be told the lonely?"

●━●━●━●

*This stems from many causes. You will find that there are
those who are lonely because they desire to be lonely, because they do not desire to reach out and touch other lives
in a meaningful way. There are also those who are lonely
because they feel they are alone, and do not have an understanding of the outer realms . . . or that God is truly
with them, and the angels or the Holy Spirit, if one would
consider another aspect.*

*You must tell them that it is necessary to begin to relate
to their fellow humans, that they find the reasons and
causes for apartness, that they integrate their own mind
and soul and self so that they can then be integrated into
the society of others; that "as they give, so shall they receive," for as they break their own tie of loneliness, they
will be able to relate to others who are in the same feeling
of emotion; and because of that, they can draw not only
themselves away from loneliness, but bring others with
them.*

*You may also be aware that there are those who mourn
the lost ones, because they feel that life is ended when it is
no longer seen on the earth-plane. This is essential that
they come to realize that there is an ongoingness, for only
as they begin to understand this more thoroughly will they
in turn be better prepared for the transition themselves.*

*It is well if, through various channels or studies, they
come to know that these "lost ones" are in a realm that is
right and good for them, one that is far greater, far more
open, far more loving and enlightening than that which
they have left. Those who mourn are many times mourn-
ing for themselves, and also that they feel the endness and
the hopelessness of life ending in death. Hope is essential,
and it must spring forth in these. "Hope and desire and
brotherhood" are all qualities which must be developed.*

Understanding is again essential, for understanding of self and others would be a basic quality *before brotherhood could be implemented.* ━━ ━━ ━━ ━━

"What can be told young adults, those who become embroiled in war?"

━━ ━━ ━━ ━━

There are those who have experienced this before, have felt the sting and the bite of war, and have seen the futility and uselessness of continuous strife. These ultimately commence the task of helping their own country and other countries to find a peaceable existence with each other so that all life might be preserved. For even that which appears to be negative life is necessary, in that those are the ones who must continue to strive upwards. You will find that this is slowly but surely coming about. It has been as a form of revolt, and yet this revolt must be brought into a peaceable demonstration; that the ways to work with each other—to learn to work from the basic human needs upward—so that governments, in essence, can begin to understand and relate to each other on a higher level.

This will have to begin with the basic people, the human needs, the desire for food and bread and water, the need for comfort and health. As these are accomplished on a worldwide basis, so will there be less anxiety and problems, or need to be aggressive and overwhelm or eat up the other.

They will need to define within themselves their own need for participation. If they feel very strongly against this, they must weigh and measure why they feel thusly. If it is from a feeling of lack, then they must face up to this, that it might be overcome. However, if they feel strongly that they can help their fellow man on another basis, or in another area, this must also be stayed with. ━━ ━━ ━━ ━━

"What about the conscientious objector, the one who states, 'I shall not kill another," yet accepts service of a non-killing nature?"

It depends a great deal on the inner workings of this particular soul. If he can truly say, "I desire to help my fellow man. I shall do all things that I can to alleviate pain and suffering. Even though I must stand by and watch my fellow man kill his neighbor, I can be there to minister to those who are hurt, regardless of the side they are on," then this one has done all that is within his own personal power to overcome a debt.

— — — — — —

"What message might help parents understand more clearly their children who develop different life-styles, different life-goals?"

— — — — — —

These same mortal parents must realize that these children have their own lives to live. They have been sent this particular bundle of joy to be able to rear it in the beginning, to provide the necessary essentials, to give it the start and the values as they were able to see them. Know that from the age of five on, those who have come are very definitely on their own, even though they are still within your care. It is necessary to allow their freedom, for through no way can you change or alter that which is basic with them. You can continue to guide or counsel, you can give help and aid as it appears necessary. However, there is a great need here for parents to draw back, for they will find that they tend to "over-give" or "over-help" certain individuals, and this does not help their growth.

You will find also that, as parents, those on the earth begin to see their own weaknesses or take the blame for that which is not their's. They must recall—and know at all times—that these children are individual souls or individual experiences for each one, and this must be allowed.

If mistakes are made, they are the burden of that particular soulchild. They can always be upheld or uplifted through thought, but they must not be manipulated through thought. You can put a layer of benevolence or help around each child and let this be the sustaining power. However, do not interfere nor manipulate them beyond that which appears to be helpful.

"What can be told others about the cycle of rebirth?"

● ▬ ● ▬ ● ▬

There are those who will not accept this as fact, and this is well, for they are not necessarily inclined to know this and it need not be there for their growth. Growth happens even as a plant comes from a seed, re-seeds itself, and again through the seed, comes back. The plant does not know this, is not aware of it, and yet the cycle goes on. Thus man is not always aware of his own cycle. There are those who have accepted reincarnation and feel that this is the "total" answer. They must be made aware that this is only one of the steps in all eternity, that there are many other planes and reaches that they must go to. Many feel that the earth-plane is the only thing they know and recognize, and can be secure in. Those who are secure are much as a babe in a playpen who is not satisfied with the world outside, for he does not recognize all of the uncharted wealth that is his to be found. As one comes forth from the playpen, they begin to see the immensity of the world around them, and once they become aware of the world, they can become more aware of the universe. Even as this is so, so the soul of man must realize that even the universe is only as a playpen to the "Total."

● ▬ ● ▬ ● ▬

I mentioned to Lenora that *The Urantia Book* described in detail what Harold and Herod were hinting at, the inconceivable magnitude of the Master Universe that contained many, many universes.

I suddenly remembered that, all too soon, Lenora and her family would be leaving, and my feelings saddened with nostalgia. No more communications, no more Herod and Harold. (As if in answer to this mood, the following suddenly and gently came through:)

● ▬ ● ▬ ● ▬

This has been one of the most meaningful that you have witnessed as yet. Much has been accomplished. Go in love and peace, knowing that all who are with you are rejoicing because of that which has come to you.

Before asking my final question, (which I'd been saving), I wanted to ask a question for all the Star Trekkers, for all science-fiction fans. "Can you tell us whether towards the more populated areas of the universe, there are such things as spaceships, real fleets of spaceships?

(A pause occurred here, almost as if private conversations were being held somewhere else. Then the following was given quite slowly:)

━ ━ ━ ━ ━

These are not unheard of . . . these are not unknown. You have touched upon it, and yet you cannot conceive in your mind's eye that which they have, for man's attempts thus far are very puny compared to those spaceships which have been created in other spheres. Do not let this trouble you, however, for you shall see these . . . in time.

━ ━ ━ ━ ━

Then I asked the last question, a request that Harold and Herod send a message to all humanity for our book. Warmly came the following:

━ ━ ━ ━ ━

There is really little one can say that will speak to all people, for each one is so individualized that the need would be varying in each case. However, we can give them the assurance that they can tell from the emotional level when there is help with them, and once they become aware of the fact that there is more to life than is met by their eyes, they will begin to feel that there is the need to reach to other planes or levels. They will not fully comprehend the immensity of it . . . may consider it to be a limited amount of an angelic kingdom or just a guardian angel with them. This is well, for we do not care whether we are recognized to the fullest degree or not. All that is hoped from our level is that man will become aware that he does have butterfly wings, and need not always crawl the earth. It will take those with imagination, those with a freedom of thought, even those with a scientific bent—as long as they are not of a closed nature—to be made aware of these other realms. You will find that as this new age becomes more of a reality, this will be accepted on a more general level.

It will be necessary to move cautiously and to evaluate each thing which is discovered without negating it. Know that it is necessary to evaluate from several standpoints, since there can be the misinterpretation. As you think on yesterday's material today, you will see different sidelights to it than you were able to see the day before. Know that you need to experiment and experience this, and yet do not move forward too rapidly. Know that the dangers which are there are those things which man brings unto himself, those things which he "desires" to see made manifest and those things which he "fears" will be made manifest. Desire and fear are the two main thought-emotions to watch in delving into other realms.

Be patient with each of those who are striving along the path. Do not even feel frustrated with those who refuse to look upwards, for their time will come. Even as some receive it at five or seven years of age, and others receive it at seventeen, still others will not have a glimpse until they are seventy or ninety. So be patient. Each will reach it in his own time.

There will be few who will become ecstatic and realize the immensity or enormity of help that is available, or the desire and care that is on this side, to help each man forward to his fullest potential. You will find that it is necessary for man alone to work through the emotional and mental planes, so that we can help them more in the higher planes. As they become aware of their shortcomings, they will find that there are ways of meditation, ways of "transcending" and rising above those problems which appear to be so tremendous to them . . . that one especially of humility, for this must be overcome before they can have the grander sight to be able to see that which is beyond. ━━━━━

I thanked them and said, "I'll miss these communications . . . " (Gently:)
━━━━━
The answers to all your questions lie within you . . .
━━━━━

Chapter X
Primary and Secondary Realities

It was unexpectedly learned during a question-answer session in 1972 that selected groups of interested people (those who have transitioned over to other realms), were gathering around whenever Lenora and I got together. Before evaluating the creative wisdom behind a planetwide amnesia factor, it could prove beneficial if the details surrounding this discovery were revealed.

I stated, "Dreams seem to occur intermixed, both positive and negative. It would be far more comfortable to us if those negative dreams disappeared . . . "

━●━●━●━

This is true, but there are those areas of the mind that are causing you to be aware of these areas as yet. Continue with diligence and you will find that this fades in time. This is the old inner self throwing up images to you, to cause a disconcerting area in your life. Do not be troubled.

━●━●━●━

"Pertaining to man's evolutionary growth, how is primitive 'burlap' transformed into robes worthy of a 'Son of God?'"

▬▬▬▬▬

The thread you speak of is not as a burlap thread—compared to the gossamer robes—but is more as a heavy cord of nylon which, through the refinement of time, becomes more as a narrow, almost invisible cord. Know that it is the same material, only refined. It is the same process, but on a higher level or plane. All things are basically of the same material, and yet each has the ability to reflect a different light, a different chord, a different time, a different feel.

▬▬▬▬▬

"But why create all these different planes and complex forces? Wouldn't it be far easier to have just one realm on each planet, and . . . ?"

▬▬▬▬▬

This is to be a creation of "perfection," and there is no need to skimp on the materials nor the "time." Know that these are things which have been for many, many, many, many, many, many, many aeons, and it is not necessary to speed up the progress. It is gradually gaining momentum and perhaps to your eyes it is imperceptible, but know that it is being done, and it "shall be."

▬▬▬▬▬

"One wonders how such vast power and creativity is hidden from man's senses? It must be the opposite view, that man's mind is like a sieve!"

▬▬▬▬▬

Much flows through his consciousness and much is non-recognized there. However, the greatest degree of this comes on the unconscious level. This is the reason that he has so many of his traumas and phobias. This is the reason that he has so many of his nervous breakdowns and so many of his problems. Many of them are not of his own making or of his own doing, only of his own receiving and not having the ability to protect himself. This has not been "taken" from him, but is not "recognized" by him. He is coming to an understanding of this, and things shall change. Know that even as you have witnessed the tremendous power that is within a seed—so that it can break through cement walks and concrete walls—even as this tiny seed is a tremendous power, so these powers which come from without are of (the magnitude of) . . . 1,000,000,000,000,000 . . . and on . . . times that in energy.

━━━━━━

"How does one protect oneself in daily life?"

━━━━━━

You will find that daily meditation can be extremely effective as a reminder to the Inner Self . . . the Higher Self remains on guard, but the Inner Self needs daily programming, daily encouragement.

━━━━━━

"There seem to be many among us who do not clearly understand, or interpret in different ways, the real meaning of Christ's mission to this planet. What can be given to clarify this issue for the many different branches of Christianity?" (With a gentle trace of sadness came the following:)

━━━━━━

These are the ones who miss the point of life that is deep within them. They need to understand that this is one who has come as a "way show-er" and a redeemer. They may not follow that one known as the Christ, but by trying to pattern their lives after this particular universal "set of values," they can then become more whole or complete themselves.

This was the sign of one who had completed a circle of incarnations and was perfect in His own being. He was with the Father from the beginning, as were all mortals, and yet few if any are able to realize that this "was" their beginning, and this "shall be" their end.

━━━━━━

We reflected on the many sayings and parables, the teachings to His own brothers and sisters to help open their eyes. And here, once again, were the seraphim, eternally dedicated to their chosen tasks of helping every man, woman, and child expand in love and understanding. Lenora and I paused to mentally thank these angelic guides for their help. Suddenly, an answer came:

There is no need . . . it is always of benefit, not only to those two who sit here, but to those who are watching on from other realms, for great growth comes through many channels. Know that as you work, you are helping others to develop, those who are unseen, unheard on your plane, in your level.

━━ ━━ ━━ ━━ ━━

"Do you mean we're not alone, that there are other observers here?"

━━ ━━ ━━ ━━ ━━

Those who have need, those in your particular group at this time appear to be about forty . . . perhaps thirty seven might be an accurate count.

━━ ━━ ━━ ━━ ━━

"Hm . . . That's a sizeable group! What can these people hope to learn from us? We have lived in total darkness as pertains to their realm."

━━ ━━ ━━ ━━ ━━

These are the ones who are closest to the physical incarnation as yet. Many of them have suffered through the very same things that you have. It is because of this that they are able to see the growth that you are making. This means that they are learning on a very elementary level, and they will then be ready to accept the position that they hold in "this" world.

They are the ones who did not delve nor dig into this in the earth incarnation, and thus their questions are numerous, even as those who yet rely on the earth for sustenance. They are brought through understanding patrons who know that it must be given in this manner, for only as they see others coping with the same problems, can they then accept the answers. If they were to look to the High Masters on this side, they would be so dazzled by the light that they would refuse to accept the answers—even as they came—feeling very unworthy to acknowledge that this is for them.

━━ ━━ ━━ ━━ ━━

"Are they interested in scientific fields, such as Time, Space, Motion, or universal concepts and meanings?"

Not necessarily. We are able to witness, or "vision," those things which have been created and are continuing. But to understand that you understand is well—to understand that you are coping with your Inner Self and are seeking to the higher realms, so that when you cross over, you will "bypass" much that is even now going on—is important for us to know and to witness. These who are here today are of a generally higher evolvement than many with whom we work. We take them to those areas where we feel the best can be given or done for that particular problem, or being. There are those to whom your mind would seem like an angelic kingdom, were you to probe their depths of darkness. These we do not bring to you—only those who are able to comprehend those areas that you speak of, are present. Know that they are those who have learned and have forgotten, and have forgotten to seek at a meaningful time in their lives. Thus it is that they are ready to receive, ready to move on, but there are some points that are necessary to be clarified for them.

"Are there educational institutions in their realm?"

Yes, but their qualifications are not as yet adequate to enter these. In due season they shall be given the opportunity.

"I take it that this isn't one of their field trips . . . like, "Let's all go visit the "funny farm" today?" Lenora laughed, said she could sense their laughter, then replied, "No, it's serious."

"Well, although we can't see you, it's a bit of an honor to us that someone would think enough of our question sessions to want to join us. I don't have any more questions for today, but we've learned much. I'm grateful . . . "

You have now stepped over the threshhold into a new room, or an inner delight. You have found that there is a great deal that can be given you daily, and this is as a food or manna for you. Continue in your searching, for there is no lack of patience with us. There is only the thought that those who are willing will turn, and as each one turns, we are indeed gratified. Be patient with yourself and others, even as we have been patient with you. Know that there is an essence in all mankind that is beauty and harmony. Know that this needs to be brought forth, and can only be done so through love and patience, through time and effort. Energy is there, but must be expelled or released. Joy is great in these other realms when new ones join the ranks of believers, of seekers. ◆◆◆◆◆

Answers to our three original questions—"What am I?" "What am I for?" and "Why?"—may be found by commencing with the timeless teaching that God is omnipotence (all potency, power and energy), omnipresence (is within and without everything everywhere), and omniscience (is all knowledge, all wisdom). Therefore, God is the 'ALL.' Such an ALL or Universal God might also be described as the Divine Collective of all intelligences in the Universe of universes, yet we know that the Whole is greater than the sum of its parts. (A poem is more than ink and paper.) Such an all-pervading boundless God may be considered limitless, timeless, and infinite, One Who's cup is full to overflowing.

To track down the "Why?" of creation, it might prove interesting to *reverse* man's usual (limited) way of trying to ascertain God's purpose. Man, being very contracted, desires only to "expand." He forever desires "more." He eternally strives to fill his half-empty cup. The *reversal* of this limited theme reveals a different situation. From the standpoint of One Who's cup is already full to overflowing, anything "more" becomes insignificant, superfluous, even redundant. Rather, such a vast Intelligence might eventually desire the exact opposite of those freedoms that man seeks to obtain; namely, *to seek defined "boundaries", to create "self-limits" within which to live, to grow, to move,* and *to have individual "being."*

How could this be accomplished? Consider the ocean as one example of *primary reality*. By the ocean's acceptance of "limits" or "boundaries" (the ocean bed below, the air above), a *tension* is created on its surface. This tension reacts in equal and opposite directions (up and down) to form a completely new phenomenon: "wave motion." These "waves" are quite real, but they are

classed as "*secondary realities.*" Waves in reality are the *ocean.*
Their existences are purely *temporary.* (The *secondary* reality of
the "audience" exists only so long as *primary* realities, *real
people*, are gathered together. When the people depart, the
audience ceases to exist.)

Observe the rolling play of the waves as they appear to travel
great distances across their source, the ocean. By the acceptance
of "self-limitations" (its surface boundary and its bottom), the
ocean has achieved a totally new mode of expression. *Through
these new "secondary realities,"* the ocean may experience the
joys of *Time-Space-Motion.* And is this all?

Consider the wave. It too has surface tension that produces
tertiary realities, or "wavelets" on the wave itself. And the
wavelet? It has surface tension also, producing ripples on its surface boundaries. And on and on it goes. It can be easily seen that
by accepting limitations, boundaries, and conditions, *an endless
series of new expressions becomes actively possible.* Even the
atom is revealed as "wave phenomena."

How might an infinite "ocean" of Consciousness limit Itself?
One subtle method might be that of immersing a spark of Its
Consciousness into an energy-field with a spherical boundary-
layer. (Perhaps a bubble will serve as a suitable analogy, if the air
within the bubble is seen as consciousness.) But such a conscious
bubble—simply knowing Itself as "I"—would not be able to
motivate Itself. By defining Itself further, by donning a second,
stronger bubble (i.e., a *denser* energy-field with stronger
boundary-layers), It can perhaps—now knowing Itself as "I
AM"—achieve a primal mode of expression; but yet without
"movement," since this necessitates something *else*—some
other *something* to move in relation *to.* Without another something nearby, there could be no way to determine self-motion.
Thus It must enfold Itself with a third, even *denser* field
boundary-layer, and It can now cognize something "other than"
Its own inner Consciousness. It can now state: "I AM *THAT.*"
When this conscious Entity creates a further expression of Itself,
by donning a fourth 'bubble,' It discovers that this next density of
energy boundary-layer *reflects* consciousness like a mirror. Gazing at this new mode of consciousness, It now states: "I AM
THAT 'I' . . . " But the situation hasn't really changed, as far as
"motion" is concerned, so It proceeds to create a state of "being"

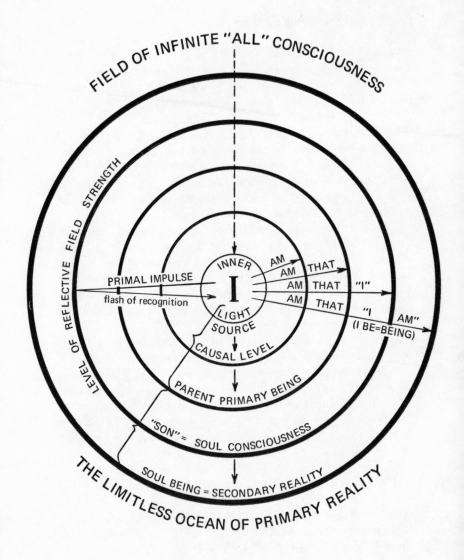

A STUDY OF SELF- INDIVIDUALIZATION:
PRIMARY - SECONDARY CREATION

for this *new secondary consciousness* by enfolding Itself in a yet *denser* field of energy, the fifth 'bubble.' Recognition of this *new secondary being* enables It to state: "I AM *THAT* 'I AM'." Or: "*I AM THAT BEING*" is the statement of the Parent-Creator that reveals *a direct relationship, the eternal link between Self and Not-self:* (the Father in the Son, and the Son in the Father.) The Two, in reality, are One. Yet one is *Source,* (or Parent), and the other is Its created, living *Reflection,* (a living Soul.) The primal "motion" can be seen as the flash of recognition between the Two. This living "flash" of the Light of Consciousness is *Spirit.* Thus is the One enabled to express Itself as the Three-in-One (Trinity) by the process of *accepting Self-limitations.* When It enfolds in even more boundary-layered energy fields, these serve as Its vehicle, a "body."

It can now be classified as a separate "Being," existing within the All Consciousness, yet apart from It, separated by interpenetrating layers of energy fields extending from the subtlest to the gross. One might note that the denser the field boundary-layer, the greater the tension-pressure and therefore the stronger the bodily structure; but because of these greater tension-pressures, the *limitations* on consciousness and body would be proportionately greater.

Then by selecting different combinations of surface "wave" vibrations, different forms and textures can be created. An inner creative Intelligence might appear outwardly disguised as a bird, a tree, a mouse, a squirrel, an elephant, a cloud, a snowflake, a rock, a human being, or anything. The quality and extent of development of the sensory systems would seem to be the determining factors in the clarity of Its perceptions, since the Inner Intelligence must perceive "through" the body's sensory "windows." And specific types of life experiences would "condition" the inner Intelligence to specific modes of thought, feeling, and value, (i.e. mouselike feelings, birdlike senses, human thoughts, angelic values). But of what relative value is *one* bird? It would seem necessary to create other birds with which to relate. And it would then become necessary to create trees in which to nest, soil for the trees to stand in, and on it would continue, ad infinitum. Quite a lovely "Game" comes into focus, if one can view such an infinite process as creative "Play." But to create and indwell such a vast number simultaneously would require a technique of "pulsing" Its Consciousness between them all, and multiplex would suffice. The marvel is this: each individual micro-sequence "mind" would have to be precisely separated and coordinated with all other micro-sequence minds (in that mental spectrum) so that no "cross-talk" interference could disrupt the operation of each individual "channel" of thought. Answers (via Lenora) indicate that the God-Spark is the Controller of Time and Space spectra.

How can all these planes coexist on this planet? In our own atmosphere we have a similar activity: the interpenetration of TV waves, radar waves, radio waves, sunlight, and sound waves, all ripple along in the same space. But no one of these affects the others because they each operate in a different wavelength spectrum. The intermixing of different wavelengths does not disturb other spectra. And, even if it were necessary to provide spatial separation, the tiny atom is likened to our solar system, containing vast areas of space within its orbital boundaries. There would seem to be more than enough room to go around.

A belief as old as mankind, rather firmly entrenched, is the accepted and unquestioned statement: "I am this body." Yet the science of biology certifies that all cells replicate (mitosis), or divide to duplicate themselves. How often? This varies, but it is known that every cell in the human body changes at least once during every seven year period of life. The body constantly changes. In juxtaposition to this constant change, one's inner identity never changes. The self-awareness, the sense of "I," remains changeless even in amnesia patients.

If the bodies we inhabit today are not the same bodies we had seven years ago, then it would seem obvious that we must be something other than our bodies. True freedom, true eternal freedom, becomes immediately apparent when one realizes that each of us is the *driver* of the body-vehicle, not the vehicle itself.

Once the separation between Self and vehicle is seen, then many of the older teachings reveal deeper, more profound meanings. Two examples are as follows: (from the wisdom of Kung Fu Masters)—"Fear and cowardice are only the *body's* wisdom as to its own weaknesses. Bravery and courage are but the *body's* wisdom as to its own strengths." Another insight: "A thousand years spent contemplating the world is worth less than one day spent observing the mind." The key within this latter gem is this: when one turns within to observe the mind, one realizes there is an active awareness of consciousness. Who is it that is aware? It is the innermost you who is aware, your *Essential True Self* who is consciously aware of the mind, which is but a reflection of the. Pure Consciousness that is your essence, your BEING.

It has been stated that the nucleus of each mind is an isolated Divine Spark of the "All Consciousness," or God Absolute. This loving, Divine God-Spark seems to have created a "reflective field" within the mind, the better to see Its image. This is recognized as self-consciousness. And to the question, "What is man for?" we can now conjecture: man functions as one necessary, reflective facet of an infinite Cosmic Mirror, in which Universal God comes to know Itself, to realize all facets of Its diverse nature.

And as each of these reflective parts becomes clearer, more polished and refined, then more perfectly can Universal God come to a realization of Its unfolding status as God Supreme—a Time-Space God—through each one of us who lives in time and space. To deny experience, then, would prevent God from total realization. Each person's efforts are said to spread waves through the universe, actually helping Cosmic Self-realization. The Time-Space God "becomes." It follows an ongoing wavepath of evolution that "It knew not" as God Absolute. The Absolute simply "IS" . . . as a still, motionless ocean.

As the ocean forms the waves, so God forms time-space beings. If each ripple is in reality the ocean, then man is the Soul-being. A Soul evidently becomes a human being when It projects Itself into a time-space framework. (This has a parallel in "Betty the mother" who projects herself onto the stage of a theater, acting for a time the *secondary life* of the heroine "Elizabeth," while her *primary ongoing life* remains forgotten in the background.)

The microscopic consciousness of each cell, multiplied by the millions of its neighboring cells, becomes one unit of a "collective organ consciousness" such as Joe's Heart, of *Reader's Digest* fame. But these subconscious clusters hardly compare with human intelligence. We may be conscious "of" certain organs, but not "as" these organs. Once again, the Whole is greater than the sum of its parts. Up in the pilot's seat, acting as the Captain of these trillions of tiny crewmembers, is something "more," someone "greater." It is not the Soul, since we are told that Soul Consciousness remains constantly aware of all Its many personalities. Yet we postulate that man *is* the eternal Soul. What are the differences between these two apparently separated levels of consciousness?

The first (and most obvious) is that the Soul remains consciously aware of Its Source. Man does not. Unlike the Soul, man lives an isolated existence in one plane and seems to have no memories of his eternal past. Also, man assumes life in one of two sexual forms, either male or female, and dons a body of a specific color, lives in a specific culture, and adopts a specific racial heritage.

New question: Does a driver of a car ever think, "Gosh! . . . My car is naked!"? Why not? Is it because he *knows* he is something "other than" the car? The Eden scene in Genesis neatly symbolizes "descent" from Soul Consciousness into bodies. Adam and Eve had no thought of nakedness (*prior* to the so-called descent, which actually occurs at birth and is more like switching television's UHF back to VHF), simply because they *knew* they were the "drivers." They clearly recognized their physical bodies for exactly what they were: "*vehicles*" in which to explore and experience the beauties of this world, in which to go anywhere they desired.

Before probing into the question of why this "descent" became necessary, it is essential to examine the key which explains this whole puzzle. *Only by blocking off all their memories of the past, of their true status, of their all-knowing Source, could they have ever come to a false belief that they were merely their body-vehicles.* And as this narrowing of conscious focus took place, one can even now imagine the surprised exclamations echoing out of the Garden, "Good heavens! . . We're naked as jaybirds!"

The real question is this: "What is the point of contracting, of leaving the Edenic state for the limitations of the flesh?" The answer lies hidden within the process of creativity. There is one particular type of being that cannot be instantly created—*an experienced person.* To gain experience, one must actually enter the time-space stream and live through the experiences. All limitations—including parental upbringing, community laws and standards, moral and educational teachings, peer group pressures—combine to produce that exquisite, unique, multi-faceted gem known as *"personality."* And what did we think a totally "impersonal" God Absolute was all along hoping to become?

What is the greatest universal adventure of all time? A gradual blending of Absolute *and* relative will unfold a God Supreme, which translates: a combined *God and person* will blossom into *a personal Time-Space God, will open the door to realization of the next stage of Godhood.*

"Man" is herein defined as: an intelligent micro-sequence of Soul Consciousness which is projected into a time-space-motion framework for the purpose of experientially evolving a personality; which occupies and operates the voluntary control systems of the body-vehicle; which uses the body's sensory mechanisms for its expressions and perceptions; which retains a reflective awareness of its "I" consciousness; and which has had all knowledge and memory of his true status and past history temporarily blocked off, (i.e., the Amnesia Factor).

A self-conscious intelligence, one whose prime function is the evolving of personality, will find it necessary to expand its Self-awareness. Man can hardly cope successfully with the demands of his environment while burdened with the incessant desires, needs, and hungers of his body-vehicle. He needs some method of lifting the strict limitations from his conscious focus, a way to re-become the "driver" instead of the slave. This would require a method of progressively refining the body's nervous system and brain, since these two form the "dark glasses" through which the inner intelligence "sees" and evaluates the environment. To successfully cope, one needs clear, balanced "glasses."

Clinical research on a broad scale suggests that Transcendental Meditation spontaneously and effortlessly produces these exact results. TM has been shown to simultaneously refine the nervous system and synchronize the brain wave function of both cerebral hemispheres. This indicates that instead of one mental "wheel" slipping in the mud with a loss of energy, TM produces a positraction effect which synchronizes and equalizes the load. TM gradually eliminates former "wheel spinning" and produces efficient forward progress.

The results to be obtained from refining one's conscious focus are an easier, more successful life, enriched senses, a greater sense of fulfillment, and the realization of each person's full potential. Rather than struggling along with merely a small percentage of one's mental capacity, full potential signifies the availability of 100 percent in all aspects of life. The profound clarity and insight of those who have reached this state in history are regarded as amazing.

Another view is that it would be quite necessary for each person to experience the *full range* of feelings, emotions, and thoughts, in order to produce a *balanced, symmetrical personality*. The sad use of power by an unbalanced personality is well understood, especially by the victims.

Additionally, the time-reactions of karma (both good and bad) are said to be slower in lower levels of consciousness, quickening as one expands the focus. It would seem advantageous to gain "time" for the growth process by starting life at an "innocent" level of consciousness, such as an amnesia patient or a newborn infant. At highest levels, karma is said to be instantaneous, and, in such an environment, one's actions would bring instant reactions. But who can know all the laws of the universe? "Spontaneous Right Action" is one benefit resulting from TM. With such an easy technique available, it is no longer necessary, nor even advisable, to be concerned with past karma. Just as stresses are dissolved, TM gradually dissolves past karma. The two are quite synonymous.

The amnesia factor also serves as a necessary safety factor. Without it, one would have memory-recall of certain power factors within each individual, the indiscriminate use of which could produce a churning chaos. Each must achieve a high degree of integrity before attaining higher consciousness, and "spontaneous right action" would seem the easiest path to try.

A powerful assist comes with the discovery that all persons on this planet were sent here from other star systems to enroll in a highly experimental "school" of rapid growth; that each man, woman, and child contains within the nucleus of the mind a priceless, sparkling *God-Spark of the Absolute Source of Creation* which is *unlimited* in potential and forms a bond of equality throughout all races, all members of humanity; and that every single one of us is equally loved and cherished by that God-Force with an intensity beyond thoughts or description.

That which words cannot describe, experience often can. TM enhances and expands all the senses and, although it is definitely not a religion (simply a deeper form of rest), it adds greater and richer values to one's inner experiences as well as one's outer activities. It is said that TM easily accomplishes this because of the existing link between rest and activity. One foot walks, the other rests. In this way, all similar cycles are linked together. The more profound the rest, the more enriched become one's experiences. And, surprisingly, these start with the first day of meditation.

When questions were asked about life on this planet and the amnesia factor as a necessary condition, Herod and Harold briefly stated:

━━━━━━

This is the way, the order, the method of ongoing, progressive growth. All levels seek to assist in this evolutionary expansion of God Supreme. They love to do this, it is a joy.

━━━━━━

Then was asked, "Is the loss of memories at birth merely a matter of taking on a new body, or is there more?"

━━━━━━

It is many times for the emotional and mental health or welfare of that particular being. There are those who are able to recall or remember, and this is when there is a definite purpose to be accomplished. However, it is not just because of the new body, but that the Soul has chosen to blind itself from past experiences so that it will be able to be more open and adjustable in the new situation.

━━━━━━

"We humans view this world as a *primary reality.* Perhaps it would be more correct to think of it as a temporary, *secondary reality,* and that our *real* life and identities originate from some other realm or star system?"

This is the way that man needs to learn to look at his own "being," for through this, he will then do the very best that he is able, in each incarnation, feeling that this is total and apart from anything else . . . for in one sense it is, and yet the Total Soul is that which lives in "all time."

━ ━ ━ ━ ━

"And this Soul remains always aware of Its eternal identity?"

━ ━ ━ ━ ━

Yes, very much so.

━ ━ ━ ━ ━

"And each of us, in reality, *is* an eternal, ongoing Soul-Being?"

━ ━ ━ ━ ━

Truer words were never spoken.

━ ━ ━ ━ ━

"How far should we expand this book? There are so many more areas."

━ ━ ━ ━ ━

Do not give them too much on a silver platter. Give them the option and the privilege of searching and seeking, so they will then have the satisfaction and pleasure of finding their own answers—of forming their own conclusions in the light of their own particular knowledge—that this might become a work of their own creation, something that reflects their own inner beauty.

━ ━ ━ ━ ━

And this ended the sessions. Lenora suddenly chased away my feeling of loss with her unforgettable exclamation, "Say! Do you realize, do you really realize what we've found? Everyone is immortal! We'll all live *forever!*"

Epilogue

Dearest Lenora,

Welcome back, strangers! Harvest time, pumpkins transform-
ing into jack-o-lanterns, and perky squirrels gathering up nuts,
tell us it's time to settle back and relax and enjoy Nature's preparations for the winter season. Is not this remarkable changing
'stage' a truly fantastic creation? Yet one discovers how easy it is
to become totally immersed (yea, trapped) in "outer" creativity.
And how easy it is to become overly fascinated by "outer" forces,
such as psychic energies and unseen phenomena. When will we
learn the final "lesson," that the wisest of the wise *first* completes
the task of turning within, of reaching and attuning to and becoming one with the Source within. Then, it has been promised,
"All these 'things' shall be added unto you." The clarity of the
teachings of Maharishi include a simile which states: 'A wise
man, one who would conquer the whole kingdom, does not
waste his time and energies conquering the outlying areas and
valuable mines therein. He proceeds via the quickest, shortest
route to the fort in the center of the kingdom, captures that, and
all the mines are then his.'

Am planning to slip once more into Nature's magic mountains,
before trout season ends. Nature is a wellspring of soothing waters, found by those who learn to listen to the silent language and
music of burbling brooks and green forests. I've finally learned
that mere words won't substitute for the *experience*, and the
same goes for just writing about fishing trips! And double for trying to describe the bliss, the relaxing peace, the new life resulting from that TM.

My best regards to your patient hubby and your four good
looking children. And take extra good care of yourself, sweet ora-
cle. God bless you forever.

Vaya con Dios,
Dad

P.S. Please tell Herod and Harold they're welcome to come
along, but only on the condition that they bait their own hooks!
Am well aware of their fishing abilities. And incidentally, they
sent me another poem. Will it ever end?

RAINBOW'S END

Searching, searching, ever outward,
Along deep ancient treks in Time;
An endless pace to find a trace
Of primal Cause, and life sublime.
Vast arching streams of energies,
The surging, heaving tides of Space;
Hurled on and down the celestial Round,
To try to glimpse the Creator's Face.
Through vortex spirals and needle points,
Dimensions spanned with burning eyes;
Hope dimming as a flickering fire,
Time held no clue, Space no surprise.
The first faint hint that one can find
Is found within reflective mind;
Gaze upon yon mirror's image,
Be still, and let life's spring unwind.
The Priceless Jewel, for which all seek,
Cannot be found on vector's line;
But there, at subtle rainbow's end,
Is Love eternal, the Spark Divine.

Bibliography

2150–The Macro Love Story, Don & Thea Plym, M.D.C., Tempe, Ariz. USA 1971

Psychic Discoveries Behind the Iron Curtain, Ostrander & Schroeder, Prentice-Hall Inc., New Jersey USA 1970

Seth Speaks, Jane Roberts, Prentice-Hall Inc., New Jersey USA 1972

Seven States of Consciousness, Anthony Campbell, Perennial Library, Harper & Row, New York USA 1974

The Brotherhood of Angels and of Men, Geoffrey Hodson, Theosophical Publishing House, London-Wheaton, Illinois USA 1957

The Kingdom of the Shining Ones, Newhouse, F.A., Christward Publications, Escondido, California USA 1955

The Kirlian Aura, Photographing the Galaxies of Life, ed. Stanley Krippner & Daniel Rubin, Anchor Press-Doubleday, Garden City, N.Y. USA 1974

The Secret Science Behind Miracles, Max Freedom Long, Huna Publications, Vista, California USA 1954

The Seth Material, Jane Roberts, Prentice-Hall Inc., New Jersey USA 1971

The Urantia Book, Urantia Foundation, Chicago, Illinois USA 1955

The Wisdom of Kung Fu, Michael Minick, William Morrow & Company Inc., New York USA 1974

Ufology, New Insights From Science and Common Sense, James M. McCampbell, Jaymac Company, Belmont, California USA 1973

Uri, Andrija Puharich, Anchor Press-Doubleday & Company Inc., Garden City, New York USA 1974 (Recent release: *My Story,* Uri Geller, Praeger, Inc., New York USA 1975.)

Note–OOBE: acronym for Out of Body Experience. An excellent report of these phenomena is found in *Journeys out of the Body,* R. A. Monroe; introduction by C. T. Tart, author of *Altered States of Consciousness* and Professor of Psychology at University of California, Davis; Anchor Press-Doubleday & Co. Inc., Garden City, New York USA 1973

Glossary

Absolute: the infinite ocean of Pure Bliss Consciousness.

All: evidently the sum total of all levels of conscious existences, all levels of energy, yet is more than the sum of Its parts.

Aura: radiance surrounding all objects. (See bibliography - Kirlian).

Betsy: a sleek Alfa Romeo fastback coupe that went too fast.

Channel: a person who has developed the "inner hearing" of the mind, just as one can "see" in the mind with one's eyes closed.

Dimension: one sector of the creative life spectrum that is said to contain seven planes, i.e. seven channels tuneable in one TV set.

Divine God-Force:

Divine God Spark:

Divine Architect:

Divine Thought Adjuster: (see *The Urantia Book,* pp. 1176–1237). these evidently refer to the living love, power, and creative wisdom of God levels of consciousness.

High Self: (Soul-being), superconscious level of mind.

IMS: International Meditation Society

Is: existential in the *primary* reality state (eternal), as contrasted with transient existence in a *secondary* reality (Time-Space).

Karma: translates: *action.* In a physics sense, like dropping a rock in a vast pond, all causal impulses are said to repercuss through all space, even through all time sequences. These impulses produce wave actions which are said to reflect back to their cause.

Laser: a high intensity beam of coherent light energy.

Level: same as "plane."

Master Architect: God as Universal Intelligence.

Mental Plane: fifth dimension; one stage beyond astral, or fourth.

Midway Translators: (see *The Urantia Book,* pp. 855–865).

Multiplex: the simultaneous broadcasting of separate signals on one frequency or along one wire. The technique is to properly sequence microseconds of the main signal into separate, organized channels.

Non-flux: same as zero density.

Plane: (also, Level)—one particular realm of life, such as our "physical plane". Although interpenetrated by other planes, each plane is said to have distinct energy-boundaries that form a framework within which people live, move, and have being. Also, a plane is similar to one TV channel.

Prana: life force, vital force, Universal in nature. Orient: *chi.*

Sims: Students' International Meditation Society

Soul-Being: (also, High Self)—the True Being, a Son of God.

Supreme: refers to Time-Space existence and evolutionary growth. Absolute "Is," the Supreme "becomes."

Transceiver: a radio unit capable of both transmitting and receiving.

UFO: Unidentified Flying Object, herein said to be a spacecraft of extraterrestrial origin. Evidence suggests there are many different design-shapes and categories of these highly maneuverable craft; also, that there have been different groups of visitors with different motives in the past.

Zero Density: any plane or level that transcends Time-Space flux. This could be likened to standing on a riverbank "out of the pressure of the flowing river.

Index